# Ego Unmasked:

# Navigating

# Authentic Living

**Vipresh Dwivedi**

# DEDICATION

This book is dedicated to its readers—the seekers, the dreamers, and the courageous souls who embark on the journey of self-discovery and growth. Your curiosity, your openness, and your willingness to explore the depths of your own being inspire the pages of this book.

To you, the reader, who bravely confronts the complexities of ego, who seeks authenticity amidst the noise of the world, and who strives for a life of purpose and meaning—this book is dedicated to you.

May the words within these pages serve as guides, companions, and sources of inspiration as you navigate the twists and turns of your own journey. May you find wisdom, clarity, and solace in the reflections offered here, and may you emerge with a deeper understanding of yourself and the world around you.

Thank you for your presence, your curiosity, and your willingness to explore the depths of your own soul. May this book accompany you on your journey of self-discovery, and may you find within its pages the guidance and inspiration you seek.

# ACKNOWLEDGEMENT

Writing this book has been a journey of introspection, growth, and discovery, and I am deeply grateful to all those who have supported and inspired me along the way.

First and foremost, I would like to express my heartfelt gratitude to my family for their unwavering love, encouragement, and understanding throughout the writing process. Your belief in me has been my greatest source of strength and inspiration.

I am indebted to my friends and colleagues who have provided invaluable feedback, encouragement, and support as I navigated the intricacies of bringing this book to life. Your insights and perspectives have enriched the pages of this book in ways I could never have imagined.

I extend my gratitude to the readers who have embraced the ideas and concepts presented in this book with openness, curiosity, and enthusiasm. Your engagement and feedback have motivated me to delve deeper into the exploration of ego, authenticity, and personal growth.

I would also like to acknowledge the countless authors, teachers, and thinkers whose wisdom and insights have informed and inspired the content of this book. Your contributions to the fields of psychology, philosophy, and spirituality have shaped my understanding and perspective in profound ways.

Finally, I offer my deepest appreciation to the dedicated team at the publishing house who have worked tirelessly to bring this book to fruition. Your passion, professionalism, and commitment to excellence have been instrumental in transforming ideas into reality.

To all those who have played a part, big or small, in the creation of this book, please accept my heartfelt thanks. May the insights and reflections shared within these pages inspire and uplift you on your own journey of self-discovery and growth.

# PROLOGUE

In the vast expanse of human experience, there exists a delicate dance between ego and authenticity—a dance that shapes our perceptions, influences our choices, and defines the essence of who we are. It is a dance as old as humanity itself, woven into the fabric of our thoughts, emotions, and interactions with the world.

In the pages that follow, we embark on a journey of exploration—a journey into the depths of the human psyche, where the shadows of ego and the light of authenticity converge and intertwine. It is a journey of self-discovery, introspection, and transformation—a journey that invites us to confront the illusions of ego and embrace the truth of our own being.

As we navigate this terrain, we encounter the many faces of ego—the inflated ego that seeks validation and dominance, the fragile ego that crumbles in the face of adversity, and the healthy ego that finds balance and harmony amidst the complexities of life. We explore the impact of ego on our relationships, our aspirations, and our pursuit of fulfillment.

But amidst the shadows of ego, there shines the radiant light of authenticity—the essence of who we truly are, beyond the masks and pretenses of the egoic mind. It is the light that guides us on our quest for meaning, purpose, and connection—a light that illuminates the path to self-discovery and inner peace.

In the pages ahead, we delve into the practices, insights, and wisdom that illuminate this path—a path of mindfulness, self-awareness, and compassion. We draw upon the teachings of ancient wisdom traditions, the insights of modern psychology, and the wisdom of our own lived experiences to unravel the mysteries of ego and authenticity.

But this journey is not one that can be undertaken alone. It is a journey that requires courage, vulnerability, and a willingness to embrace the fullness of our humanity. It is a journey that we embark upon together, as fellow travelers on the path to self-discovery and awakening.

As we turn the page and begin this journey together, let us approach it with open hearts and open minds. Let us be curious, courageous, and compassionate as we explore the depths of our own being. And may this journey be a source of inspiration, insight, and transformation for us all.

Welcome to the dance of ego and authenticity. The stage is set, the music begins to play, and the journey awaits. Let us begin.

# Contents

# PREFACE

Welcome to the pages of this book, a journey into the intricate interplay between ego and authenticity—a journey that invites reflection, exploration, and transformation. As we embark on this odyssey, let us pause to consider the significance of the terrain we are about to traverse.

The concept of ego has long fascinated and perplexed humanity. From the ancient wisdom of Eastern philosophies to the modern insights of psychology, the ego has been explored, dissected, and debated. It is a concept that eludes simple definition, encompassing the myriad facets of human identity, perception, and consciousness.

In the pages ahead, we delve into the complexities of ego—the inflated ego that seeks validation and control, the fragile ego that recoils from vulnerability and uncertainty, and the healthy ego that finds balance and authenticity amidst the chaos of life. We examine the ways in which ego shapes our thoughts, influences our behaviors, and colors our perceptions of self and others.

But amidst the labyrinth of ego, there shines the beacon of authenticity—a guiding light that illuminates the path to self-discovery and inner peace. Authenticity is the essence of who we truly are, beyond the masks and pretenses of the egoic mind. It is the wellspring of joy, fulfillment, and connection—a source of strength and resilience in the face of life's challenges.

In the pages ahead, we explore the practices, insights, and wisdom that can help us navigate the landscape of ego and authenticity. From mindfulness meditation to self-reflection, from cultivating empathy to embracing vulnerability, we draw upon a rich tapestry of teachings and traditions to guide us on our journey.

But let us be clear: this journey is not one of easy answers or quick fixes. It is a journey of self-discovery, introspection, and growth— a journey that requires courage, humility, and an unwavering commitment to truth. It is a journey that we undertake not as passive observers, but as active participants in the unfolding drama of our own lives.

As we turn the page and begin this journey together, let us do so with open minds and open hearts. Let us approach each chapter with curiosity, compassion, and a willingness to challenge our assumptions and beliefs. And may this journey be a source of inspiration, insight, and transformation for us all.

So, dear reader, I invite you to embark on this adventure with me. Let us explore the depths of ego and authenticity, and may we emerge on the other side with a deeper understanding of ourselves and the world around us.

# Chapter 1: Introduction to Ego

In the intricate labyrinth of human psychology, the concept of ego stands as a towering edifice, shaping perceptions, actions, and relationships. It is the invisible force that whispers in our minds, defining who we are, how we relate to the world, and the narratives we craft about ourselves. An introduction to ego is akin to peering into the inner workings of the human psyche, unraveling its complexities and contradictions.

Ego, in its essence, embodies the sense of self, the "I" that distinguishes one individual from another. Rooted in

Freudian theory, ego represents the conscious mind's interface with reality, mediating between primal instincts and societal norms. It is the guardian of the self, navigating the terrain of desires, fears, and aspirations.

Yet, ego transcends mere psychological constructs; it permeates every facet of human existence, from personal ambitions to collective identities. It manifests in displays of confidence, insecurity, arrogance, and humility, shaping our interactions and influencing our destinies.

Exploring the contours of ego entails a journey into the depths of human consciousness, confronting the shadows lurking within and the illusions we weave around ourselves. It beckons us to confront our vulnerabilities, dismantle our defenses, and embrace the fluidity of identity.

In this introduction to ego, we embark on a quest for self-discovery, traversing the landscapes of egoism and altruism, narcissism and empathy. It is a journey fraught with paradoxes and revelations, inviting us to confront the mirrors of our own reflection and to transcend the confines of the self.

## Defining ego and its origins

At the heart of human psychology lies the intricate concept of ego, a multifaceted construct that shapes our perceptions, motivations, and interactions with the world. To define ego is to delve into the depths of consciousness, unraveling its origins and complexities that have intrigued philosophers, psychologists, and thinkers throughout the ages.

Ego, derived from the Latin word for "I," represents the nucleus of individual identity—the cohesive sense of self that distinguishes one person from another. Its origins can be traced back to the pioneering work of Sigmund Freud, the founder of psychoanalytic theory. Freud conceptualized the ego as one of the three components of the psyche, alongside the id and superego, forming the structural framework of personality.

According to Freud, the ego emerges in infancy as a response to the demands of reality, serving as the conscious mediator between the instinctual drives of the id and the moral constraints of the superego. It operates on the principle of reality, striving to balance the conflicting demands of primal desires and societal norms. Through processes such as rationalization, repression, and defense mechanisms, the ego navigates the complexities of the human experience, seeking to maintain psychic equilibrium amidst internal and external pressures.

However, the roots of ego extend beyond Freudian theory, encompassing a rich tapestry of philosophical and spiritual traditions from around the world. In Eastern philosophy, the concept of ego is synonymous with the "false self," the illusory construct that obscures the true nature of existence. Influenced by Eastern thought, Western psychologists such as Carl Jung expanded upon Freud's model of the psyche, introducing the notion of the collective unconscious and archetypes that shape human behavior.

Contemporary psychological perspectives offer nuanced interpretations of ego, acknowledging its adaptive functions while also exploring its darker manifestations. From humanistic theories emphasizing self-actualization to existentialist philosophies grappling with the search for meaning, the concept of ego continues to evolve in response to diverse cultural, social, and scientific currents.

Defining ego transcends mere intellectual inquiry—it invites us to confront the fundamental questions of identity, agency, and purpose that lie at the core of human existence. As we unravel the origins and complexities of ego, we embark on a profound journey of self-discovery, navigating the intricate interplay between individuality and interconnectedness that defines the human condition.

## The role of ego in our lives

The role of ego in our lives is both profound and pervasive, shaping our perceptions, motivations, and relationships in profound ways. At its core, ego serves as the custodian of our individual identity, the lens through which we interpret the world and construct our sense of self.

One of the primary functions of ego is to navigate the intricate terrain of human relationships. It serves as a filter through which we process interactions with others, influencing how we perceive ourselves in relation to them. Ego can manifest in various forms, from the healthy assertion of boundaries and self-esteem to the toxic dynamics of competition and superiority. In both personal and professional contexts, ego plays a pivotal role in shaping the dynamics of power, status, and belonging.

Moreover, ego serves as the driving force behind our ambitions and aspirations. It fuels the pursuit of success, recognition, and validation, propelling us to achieve our goals and fulfill our potential. However, unchecked ego can also lead to hubris and arrogance, blinding us to our limitations and undermining our relationships and achievements.

Ego plays a crucial role in our psychological resilience and well-being. It acts as a buffer against the existential anxieties and uncertainties of life, providing a sense of continuity and coherence amidst adversity. By defending against threats to our self-image and preserving a semblance of control, ego enables us to navigate the complexities of existence with a measure of equanimity.

Yet, the shadow side of ego cannot be ignored. It is often the source of inner conflict, as we grapple with competing desires, insecurities, and fears. Ego-driven attachments to material possessions, social status, and external validation can obscure deeper truths and impede our capacity for genuine connection and fulfillment.

The role of ego in our lives is multifaceted

and paradoxical. It is both the source of our individuality and the barrier to our interconnectedness with others and the world around us. Recognizing the influence of ego and cultivating self-awareness are essential steps in transcending its limitations and fostering deeper levels of authenticity, empathy, and compassion. As we navigate the complexities of the human experience, may we strive to harness the power of ego as a catalyst for growth, wisdom, and profound transformation.

## How ego affects our thoughts and actions

Ego exerts a profound influence on our thoughts and actions, permeating every aspect of our lives with its subtle yet pervasive presence. From the mundane decisions of daily existence to the profound existential questions that shape our journey, ego serves as the invisible hand guiding our perceptions, motivations, and behaviors.

At its core, ego is the lens through which we interpret the world, filtering our experiences through the prism of self-awareness and identity. It colors our perceptions, distorting reality to conform to our preconceived notions, biases, and desires. In the realm of cognition, ego manifests as the inner voice that narrates our lives, shaping the stories we tell ourselves about who we are, what we value, and what we aspire to become.

Moreover, ego plays a pivotal role in shaping our beliefs and attitudes. It fosters a sense of certainty and conviction, anchoring us to ideologies, dogmas, and worldviews that validate our sense of self and reinforce our sense of belonging. However, ego's attachment to these beliefs can also blind us to alternative perspectives and stifle intellectual curiosity, impeding our capacity for growth and self-discovery.

In the realm of emotion, ego fuels the fires of desire, fear, and aversion that drive our actions. It seeks pleasure and avoids pain, pursuing gratification and validation at the expense of deeper fulfillment and meaning. Ego-driven emotions such as pride, envy, and resentment can distort our perceptions and lead to destructive patterns of behavior, damaging relationships and undermining our well-being.

Ego influences our interpersonal dynamics, shaping the way we relate to others and navigate social hierarchies. It drives the need for validation and recognition, fueling competitions for status and dominance while fostering envy and resentment towards those perceived as threats or rivals. Ego-driven interactions often devolve into power struggles and conflicts, perpetuating cycles of aggression and alienation that hinder genuine connection and empathy.

Ego's influence on our thoughts and actions is both subtle and profound. It shapes the contours of our consciousness, coloring our perceptions, beliefs, and emotions with its distinct imprint. Yet, by cultivating self-awareness and mindfulness, we can begin to unravel the grip of ego, transcending its limitations and opening ourselves to the boundless possibilities of the present moment. As we journey towards greater clarity and insight, may we strive to align our thoughts and actions with the deeper currents of wisdom and compassion that flow beneath the surface of ego's turbulent waters.

# Chapter 2: The Development of Ego

The development of ego marks a pivotal stage in the intricate journey of human growth and self-awareness. It is a process shaped by a myriad of influences, from the earliest moments of infancy to the complexities of adult life. Understanding the evolution of ego entails delving into the interplay of psychological, social, and cultural forces that mold our sense of self and shape our interactions with the world.

In its essence, the development of ego begins in infancy, as the nascent consciousness emerges from the primordial depths of the psyche. Drawing upon the pioneering insights of psychologists such as Sigmund Freud and Erik Erikson, we trace the unfolding of ego through the stages of psychosocial development, from the struggle for autonomy and identity in childhood to the quest for intimacy and generativity in adulthood.

Central to the development of ego is the dynamic interplay between internal drives and external realities. Infants navigate the world through a process of trial and error, learning to distinguish self from other and to assert their individuality amidst the flux of sensory experiences. As they grow and mature, children internalize social norms and cultural values, shaping their identities in relation to familial, societal, and historical contexts.

The development of ego is inherently relational, forged through interactions with caregivers, peers, and broader social networks. Attachment theory illuminates the profound impact of early relationships on the formation of ego, highlighting the importance of secure bonds and emotional attunement in fostering resilience and self-regulation.

Yet, the journey of ego development is not without its challenges and conflicts. Adolescence emerges as a crucible of identity formation, as young people grapple with questions of belonging, purpose, and self-expression. The transition to adulthood brings new complexities and responsibilities, as individuals navigate the demands of work, relationships, and existential meaning.

In this introduction to the development of ego, we embark on a multidimensional exploration of the human psyche, charting the contours of growth, transformation, and self-discovery. As we unravel the mysteries of ego development, we gain insight into the intricate tapestry of human experience, and the profound potential for growth and fulfillment that lies within each of us.

## The influence of childhood experiences on ego formation

The formation of ego, that intricate construct at the core of human identity, is profoundly influenced by the kaleidoscope of experiences that shape childhood. From the tender embrace of caregivers to the challenges and adversities encountered in

the social milieu, early life experiences lay
the foundation for the development of
the self in ways that reverberate
throughout the lifespan.

At the heart of this influence lies the
dynamic interplay between attachment
and exploration, two fundamental
processes that characterize early
development. Attachment, rooted in the
primal need for security and connection,
forms the cornerstone of ego formation.
Infants and young children rely on
caregivers to meet their basic needs and
provide emotional nourishment, fostering
a sense of safety and trust essential for
healthy ego development. Consistent
responsiveness and affectionate
caregiving promote the emergence of a
secure attachment style, characterized by
a balanced sense of autonomy and

intimacy.

Conversely, experiences of neglect, abuse, or inconsistent caregiving can disrupt the formation of secure attachments, casting shadows of insecurity and mistrust that echo into adulthood. Children who grow up in environments marked by trauma or relational turmoil may develop defensive strategies to cope with perceived threats to their well-being, leading to the emergence of maladaptive ego patterns characterized by rigidity, defensiveness, or emotional dysregulation.

Moreover, the influence of childhood experiences extends beyond the realm of attachment to encompass a myriad of social, cultural, and environmental factors. Peers, teachers, and societal institutions serve as potent agents of socialization, transmitting implicit norms, values, and expectations that shape children's sense of self and others. The messages conveyed by family, media, and cultural narratives contribute to the internalization of gender roles, ethnic identities, and societal ideals, influencing the formation of ego identities that reflect broader socio-cultural contexts.

The influence of childhood experiences on ego formation embodies a complex interplay of nature and nurture, shaping the trajectory of human development in profound and enduring ways. By unraveling the intricate threads of early experiences, we gain insight into the origins of ego and the dynamic processes that underlie its formation. As we strive to understand the complexities of human identity, may we approach with empathy and curiosity, recognizing the resilience and vulnerability inherent in the journey from infancy to adulthood.

## The impact of societal and cultural norms on ego development

Societal and cultural norms exert a profound influence on the development of ego, shaping individuals' perceptions, values, and identities within the broader fabric of society. From the moment of birth, individuals are immersed in a complex web of social expectations, cultural traditions, and collective beliefs that inform their sense of self and shape their interactions with others.

At the heart of this influence lies the

process of socialization, through which individuals internalize the norms, values, and behaviors deemed appropriate within their cultural context. Family, peers, media, and educational institutions serve as primary agents of socialization, transmitting implicit and explicit messages about identity, morality, and social roles from one generation to the next.

Societal norms dictate the acceptable standards of behavior, appearance, and achievement within a given community or society. They define the boundaries of social acceptance and deviance, shaping individuals' perceptions of themselves and others. From gender roles and expectations to notions of success and failure, societal norms provide a blueprint for ego development, guiding individuals' aspirations, decisions, and self-concept.

Cultural norms, rooted in the shared beliefs, practices, and symbols of a particular group or community, further shape individuals' identities and worldview. Cultural norms encompass a broad spectrum of dimensions, including language, religion, customs, and traditions, each contributing to the richness and diversity of human experience. Through rituals, ceremonies, and rites of passage, cultures imbue life with meaning and significance, fostering a sense of belonging and continuity across generations.

However, the impact of societal and cultural norms on ego development is not uniform or deterministic. Individuals navigate a complex interplay of conformity and resistance, negotiation and adaptation, as they reconcile personal aspirations with societal expectations. Cultural diversity and globalization further complicate this dynamic, exposing individuals to a multiplicity of cultural influences and identities that shape their sense of self in increasingly fluid and hybrid ways.

Moreover, societal and cultural norms are not static entities but evolve over time in response to social, political, and economic forces. As societies undergo periods of upheaval and transformation, norms may shift, giving rise to new forms of identity and collective consciousness. In this ever-changing landscape, individuals grapple with questions of authenticity, agency, and belonging, forging unique paths of self-discovery amidst the currents of cultural change.

The impact of societal and cultural norms on ego development underscores the interconnectedness of individual and collective identity. As we navigate the complexities of modern life, may we approach the exploration of self with openness and curiosity, embracing the diversity of human experience and the transformative power of cultural dialogue and exchange.

## Nature vs. nurture: Is ego innate or learned?

The age-old debate surrounding nature versus nurture lies at the heart of understanding the development of ego—whether it is primarily innate or learned through environmental influences. Ego, as the core of individual identity and self-awareness, is shaped by a complex interplay of genetic predispositions and environmental factors, making it challenging to attribute its formation solely to either nature or nurture.

On one hand, proponents of the nature argument assert that aspects of ego, such as temperament and personality traits, have a genetic basis inherited from one's biological parents. Research in behavioral genetics has uncovered evidence of heritability for certain personality dimensions, suggesting that genetic variations contribute to individual differences in ego formation. For example, studies have identified genetic markers associated with traits like extraversion, neuroticism, and conscientiousness, which play a role in shaping how individuals perceive themselves and interact with the world.

However, the influence of genetics on ego development does not operate in isolation. Environmental factors play a crucial role in modulating genetic expression and shaping the trajectory of ego formation. From the moment of birth, infants are immersed in a complex array of social, cultural, and familial influences that shape their sense of self and interpersonal relationships. Parenting styles, attachment experiences, cultural norms, and socioeconomic status all contribute to the socialization process, influencing the development of ego structures and coping mechanisms.

The dynamic interplay between nature and nurture extends beyond infancy into childhood, adolescence, and adulthood. As individuals navigate the challenges and opportunities of different life stages, they continue to be shaped by genetic predispositions and environmental influences. Experiences of trauma, adversity, and socialization shape ego development in profound and enduring ways, influencing how individuals perceive themselves, relate to others, and navigate the complexities of human existence.

The debate over whether ego is innate or learned is a false dichotomy that fails to capture the complexity of human development. Ego formation is a multifaceted process shaped by the interaction of genetic, biological, psychological, and social factors. While genetic predispositions may set the stage for certain personality traits and temperaments, environmental influences play a critical role in sculpting the contours of ego identity and expression. By acknowledging the intertwined nature of nature and nurture, we gain a deeper understanding of the dynamic forces that shape human personality and behavior, illuminating pathways for personal growth, resilience, and self-discovery.

# Chapter 3: The Different Types of Ego

In the labyrinthine landscape of human psychology, the concept of ego unfolds as a multifaceted prism, refracting diverse shades of self-awareness, identity, and perception. As individuals navigate the complexities of existence, various typologies of ego emerge, each bearing its unique imprint on thoughts, emotions, and behaviors. Understanding the different types of ego illuminates the intricate tapestry of human experience, offering insight into the myriad ways individuals engage with themselves and the world around them.

At its core, ego represents the nucleus of

individual identity—the cohesive sense of self that distinguishes one person from another. Yet, within this overarching framework, diverse manifestations of ego surface, reflecting the kaleidoscope of human temperament, socialization, and cultural context. From the assertive confidence of a healthy ego to the fragility of an injured one, the spectrum of ego types encompasses a rich array of nuances and complexities.

One prominent typology of ego revolves around Freud's psychoanalytic theory, which delineates the id, ego, and superego as distinct components of the psyche. Within this framework, the ego serves as the conscious mediator between the primal instincts of the id and the moral injunctions of the superego, navigating the demands of reality with rationality and discretion.

Beyond Freudian theory, contemporary psychology and spiritual traditions offer additional perspectives on ego diversity. Psychologists such as Carl Jung expanded upon Freud's model, introducing concepts like the persona, shadow, and collective unconscious to elucidate the multifaceted nature of ego identity.

Moreover, Eastern philosophies and mindfulness traditions shed light on the illusory nature of ego and its myriad manifestations. From the inflated grandiosity of the egoic mind to the dissolution of self in states of egolessness, these traditions offer pathways to transcend the limitations of ego identity and cultivate deeper levels of awareness and interconnectedness.

Exploring the different types of ego invites us on a journey of self-discovery and introspection, challenging us to confront the myriad facets of our own identity and consciousness. By embracing the diversity of ego experiences, we deepen our understanding of human nature and nurture compassion and empathy for ourselves and others. As we navigate the labyrinth of ego, may we approach with curiosity and humility, recognizing the inherent complexity and beauty of the human psyche.

## The inflated ego: Signs and consequences

The inflated ego stands as a formidable

presence within the intricate landscape of human psychology, characterized by an exaggerated sense of self-importance, grandiosity, and superiority. As individuals succumb to the seductive allure of ego inflation, subtle signs and profound consequences permeate their lives, shaping relationships, aspirations, and perceptions in profound ways.

One of the hallmark signs of an inflated ego is an incessant need for validation and admiration. Individuals with inflated egos often seek external affirmation to bolster their fragile sense of self-worth, craving attention, praise, and recognition at every turn. They may resort to self-aggrandizement, boasting about their accomplishments, talents, or possessions in a bid to bolster their perceived status and superiority.

An inflated ego often manifests in a sense of entitlement and arrogance, marked by a disdain for criticism or dissenting viewpoints. Individuals with inflated egos may exhibit a sense of entitlement, expecting special treatment or privileges without regard for the needs or perspectives of others. They may dismiss feedback or constructive criticism, viewing it as a threat to their inflated self-image and resorting to defensiveness or aggression to preserve their illusion of invulnerability.

The consequences of an inflated ego extend far beyond the realm of individual behavior, permeating interpersonal relationships and social dynamics. Inflated egos can fuel conflicts, power struggles, and interpersonal tensions, undermining trust, empathy, and collaboration within personal and professional spheres. They may alienate others with their condescension, arrogance, or disregard for boundaries, fostering resentment and discord in their wake.

An inflated ego can impede personal growth and self-awareness, obscuring the individual's ability to acknowledge and learn from their mistakes or shortcomings. By clinging to a façade of perfection and infallibility, individuals with inflated egos may resist introspection and vulnerability, depriving themselves of opportunities for growth, resilience, and genuine connection.

Ultimately, the consequences of an inflated ego are profound and far-reaching, eroding the fabric of relationships, inhibiting personal development, and fostering a climate of discord and isolation. However, by cultivating humility, empathy, and self-awareness, individuals can transcend the limitations of ego inflation, fostering deeper connections, resilience, and authenticity in their interactions with themselves and others. As we navigate the complexities of the human psyche, may we strive to temper the seductive allure of ego inflation with the transformative power of humility and empathy, embracing the richness and vulnerability of the human experience.

## The fragile ego: Causes and effects

The fragile ego represents a delicate construct within the human psyche, susceptible to the slightest tremors of doubt, criticism, or adversity. Characterized by a heightened sensitivity to perceived threats to self-esteem and identity, the fragile ego manifests in a constellation of behaviors and emotional responses that reflect deep-seated insecurities and vulnerabilities.

At its core, the fragile ego often stems from early childhood experiences marked by trauma, neglect, or invalidation. Children who grow up in environments characterized by inconsistent caregiving, criticism, or emotional abandonment may internalize beliefs of unworthiness and inadequacy, laying the groundwork for a fragile sense of self in adulthood. Moreover, societal and cultural influences, such as unrealistic standards of beauty, success, and achievement, can exacerbate feelings of inadequacy and fuel the relentless pursuit of external validation.

The consequences of a fragile ego reverberate across various domains of life, affecting relationships, career aspirations, and emotional well-being. In interpersonal interactions, individuals with a fragile ego may exhibit hypersensitivity to perceived slights or rejections, leading to defensiveness, withdrawal, or passive-aggressive behavior. The fear of rejection or failure can constrain their ability to form authentic connections and engage in healthy conflict resolution, perpetuating cycles of isolation and loneliness.

Furthermore, the fragile ego often manifests in perfectionism and chronic self-doubt, as individuals strive to meet unattainable standards of excellence in a quest for validation and acceptance. The relentless pursuit of external approval becomes a Sisyphean task, fueling anxiety, depression, and burnout as individuals grapple with the relentless demands of their inner critic.

In the professional realm, the fragile ego may manifest as a fear of failure or imposter syndrome, undermining confidence and stifling career advancement. Individuals may shy away from challenges or opportunities for growth, fearing exposure or judgment from others. Consequently, they may remain stuck in stagnant roles or settle for mediocrity, resigning themselves to a life of unfulfilled potential and regret.

Understanding the causes and effects of

the fragile ego illuminates the intricate interplay of internal and external forces that shape human identity and resilience. By cultivating self-awareness, compassion, and resilience, individuals can begin to dismantle the walls of insecurity and self-doubt, fostering a more authentic and empowered sense of self. Through introspection and healing, they can embrace vulnerability as a source of strength and forge deeper connections with themselves and others, transcending the limitations of the fragile ego to embrace the fullness of their humanity.

## The healthy ego: Characteristics and benefits

The healthy ego stands as a beacon of psychological resilience and self-awareness, embodying a balanced sense of self-confidence, authenticity, and emotional regulation. Rooted in a secure attachment to reality and a robust sense of identity, the healthy ego manifests in a constellation of characteristics and behaviors that foster personal growth, meaningful relationships, and overall well-being.

One hallmark of the healthy ego is a strong sense of self-esteem that is grounded in internal validation rather than external praise or validation. Individuals with a healthy ego possess a deep-seated belief in their own worth and capabilities, allowing them to navigate life's challenges with confidence and resilience. They are able to acknowledge their strengths and limitations, embracing imperfection as an integral part of the human experience.

Individuals with a healthy ego exhibit emotional resilience and flexibility in the face of adversity. They are adept at regulating their emotions and coping with stressors in adaptive ways, rather than succumbing to destructive patterns of avoidance or denial. Instead of viewing setbacks as insurmountable obstacles, they perceive them as opportunities for growth and learning, cultivating a sense of optimism and perseverance in the face of adversity.

Authenticity and integrity are also hallmarks of the healthy ego. Individuals with a healthy ego are able to express their thoughts, feelings, and values authentically, without pretense or self-deception. They have a strong sense of personal agency and autonomy, allowing them to make choices that align with their core beliefs and values, even in the face of external pressure or disapproval.

The healthy ego fosters empathy and compassion towards others, facilitating meaningful connections and fostering a sense of belonging and community. Individuals with a healthy ego are able to recognize and validate the experiences and perspectives of others, cultivating deep and fulfilling relationships built on mutual respect and understanding.

The benefits of a healthy ego extend far beyond individual well-being, permeating every facet of life—from personal relationships to professional success and societal engagement. Individuals with a healthy ego are more likely to experience greater satisfaction and fulfillment in their personal and professional lives, as they are able to navigate the complexities of human relationships and societal expectations with grace and resilience.

The healthy ego represents a cornerstone of psychological well-being and personal growth, enabling individuals to navigate the vicissitudes of life with confidence, authenticity, and compassion. By cultivating self-awareness, resilience, and empathy, individuals can foster a healthy ego that serves as a foundation for a life of purpose, meaning, and fulfillment.

# Chapter 4: Ego and Relationships

In the intricate dance of human interaction, the concept of ego emerges as a central protagonist, shaping the dynamics, complexities, and nuances of relationships. Ego, the core of individual identity and self-awareness, weaves its threads into the fabric of interpersonal connections, influencing perceptions, behaviors, and emotional landscapes. Exploring the interplay between ego and relationships unveils a rich tapestry of intimacy, vulnerability, and growth, illuminating the myriad ways in which individuals navigate the terrain of connection and belonging.

At its essence, ego represents the lens through which individuals perceive themselves and others within the context of relationships. It encompasses the intricate interplay of self-esteem, identity, and emotional resilience, coloring the nuances of communication, intimacy, and conflict resolution. From the delicate balance of assertiveness and empathy to the vulnerabilities of intimacy and trust, ego shapes the contours of relational dynamics in profound and enduring ways.

Moreover, the influence of ego extends beyond the individual to encompass the collective dynamics of partnerships, friendships, and familial bonds. In romantic relationships, ego often manifests in patterns of attachment, communication styles, and power dynamics that shape the quality and longevity of partnerships. In friendships, ego influences the dynamics of reciprocity, support, and mutual understanding that underpin meaningful connections. In familial relationships, ego influences the roles, expectations, and boundaries that define the contours of kinship and belonging.

Yet, the interplay between ego and relationships is not without its complexities and challenges. Ego-driven conflicts, insecurities, and power struggles can undermine the foundations of trust and intimacy, eroding the bonds of connection and understanding. Conversely, healthy ego boundaries, empathy, and emotional attunement can foster resilience, authenticity, and mutual respect, enriching the tapestry of human connection with depth and meaning.

Exploring the nexus of ego and relationships invites us on a journey of self-discovery and relational exploration, challenging us to confront the complexities of intimacy and vulnerability with courage and compassion. As we navigate the intricacies of human connection, may we cultivate the wisdom and humility to navigate the terrain of ego with grace and authenticity, fostering relationships that nurture the soul and illuminate the path to deeper understanding and fulfillment.

## The role of ego in romantic relationships

In the intricate tapestry of romantic relationships, the role of ego emerges as a potent force, shaping the dynamics of intimacy, communication, and conflict resolution. Ego, the core of individual identity and self-awareness, intertwines with the complexities of love, desire, and attachment, influencing the quality and longevity of partnerships in profound ways.

At its core, ego influences the ways in which individuals perceive themselves and their partners within the context of romantic relationships. It encompasses a delicate balance of self-esteem, identity, and emotional resilience, shaping the narratives we construct about ourselves and others. Ego plays a pivotal role in the initial stages of attraction and courtship, influencing the ways in which individuals present themselves and seek validation from their partners.

Moreover, ego influences the dynamics of power and control within romantic relationships. Insecure egos may manifest in patterns of jealousy, possessiveness, and manipulation as individuals seek to protect their sense of self-worth and identity. Conversely, healthy ego boundaries facilitate mutual respect, autonomy, and trust, creating a foundation for intimacy and partnership.

Communication patterns in romantic relationships are also deeply influenced by ego dynamics. Insecure egos may lead to defensive communication styles, characterized by deflection, blame, and avoidance of vulnerability. Conversely, individuals with secure egos are more likely to engage in open, honest communication, fostering emotional intimacy and understanding.

Conflict resolution is another arena where ego plays a pivotal role in romantic relationships. Insecure egos may escalate conflicts, seeking to assert dominance or avoid feelings of vulnerability. Healthy ego boundaries, on the other hand, enable individuals to approach conflicts with empathy, flexibility, and a willingness to compromise, fostering resilience and growth within the relationship.

Ego influences the ways in which individuals navigate the complexities of intimacy and commitment in romantic relationships. Insecure egos may struggle with feelings of inadequacy or fear of rejection, leading to patterns of emotional withdrawal or avoidance of intimacy. Healthy ego boundaries enable individuals to embrace vulnerability, authenticity, and emotional connection, fostering deeper levels of intimacy and fulfillment.

The role of ego in romantic relationships is multifaceted and complex, encompassing a delicate interplay of self-esteem, identity, and emotional resilience. By cultivating self-awareness, empathy, and communication skills, individuals can navigate the terrain of ego with grace and authenticity, fostering relationships that nurture the soul and illuminate the path to deeper understanding and fulfillment.

## Ego clashes in friendships and family dynamics

Ego clashes in friendships and family dynamics unfold as intricate dramas, where the delicate balance of individual identities, expectations, and interpersonal connections meets the complexities of human emotions. These clashes, often rooted in differing perspectives, values, or needs, can strain relationships, creating rifts that demand delicate navigation and empathetic understanding.

Within the sphere of friendships, ego clashes may emerge as friends navigate the terrain of shared experiences, individual growth, and evolving priorities. Divergent life paths or changing personal values can create friction, triggering ego-driven conflicts. When one friend perceives their needs or expectations as unmet, ego defenses may surface, leading to misunderstandings, resentment, or a sense of betrayal. Navigating such clashes requires open communication, empathy, and a willingness to understand and respect each other's evolving identities.

Similarly, within family dynamics, ego clashes often arise from the intricate interplay of roles, expectations, and generational differences. Sibling rivalries, parent-child conflicts, or disagreements among extended family members can become fertile grounds for ego clashes. The struggle for recognition, autonomy, or the imposition of familial expectations can trigger defensive responses, leading to strained relationships and emotional turmoil. Navigating these clashes necessitates a delicate balance between asserting individual identity and fostering a sense of familial unity through open communication and mutual respect.

Ego clashes in both friendships and family

dynamics can be exacerbated by unmet needs for validation, recognition, or understanding. In the heat of conflict, individuals may find their egos entangled in a battle for acknowledgment or perceived fairness, potentially escalating tensions. Recognizing the underlying emotional needs and vulnerabilities that fuel ego clashes is crucial for fostering empathy and finding constructive resolutions.

The consequences of unresolved ego clashes in these relationships can be significant. Lingering tensions may erode trust, communication channels, and the emotional bonds that form the foundation of healthy connections. Persistent ego clashes can lead to estrangement, creating emotional distance and rupturing the fabric of familial or friendship ties.

Yet, within the challenges posed by ego clashes lies the opportunity for growth and transformation. Confronting these clashes with self-awareness, humility, and a commitment to understanding the perspectives of others can pave the way for healing and strengthened connections. Successful navigation of ego clashes involves fostering a culture of open communication, active listening, and mutual respect, creating a foundation for resilient relationships that withstand the tests of time and evolving circumstances.

Ego clashes in friendships and family dynamics are an inherent part of the human experience, reflective of the intricate dance between individual identities and the shared narratives of relationships. By approaching these clashes with empathy, patience, and a commitment to understanding, individuals can transform conflicts into opportunities for deeper connection and mutual growth within the intricate tapestry of their interpersonal bonds.

## How to maintain a healthy balance of ego in relationships

Maintaining a healthy balance of ego in relationships is essential for fostering intimacy, trust, and mutual respect. Striking this balance requires self-awareness, empathy, and a willingness to prioritize the well-being of both oneself and others. Here are some strategies for cultivating a healthy balance of ego in relationships:

Practice Self-Awareness: Cultivate a deep understanding of your own ego tendencies, triggers, and vulnerabilities. Reflect on your patterns of behavior, communication style, and emotional responses within relationships. Recognize the impact of ego on your interactions with others and strive to develop insight into how your ego influences your thoughts, feelings, and actions.

Cultivate Empathy: Foster empathy and compassion towards others by seeking to understand their perspectives, experiences, and emotions. Practice active listening and genuine curiosity about the thoughts and feelings of your friends, family members, and romantic partners. Empathy allows you to connect authentically with others, fostering deeper levels of understanding and intimacy within relationships.

Practice Humility: Embrace humility as a guiding principle in your interactions with others. Recognize that no one is infallible, and we all have areas for growth and improvement. Be open to feedback, constructive criticism, and differing viewpoints, recognizing that humility fosters a spirit of collaboration, learning, and growth within relationships.

Set Healthy Boundaries: Establish clear and healthy boundaries that honor your needs, values, and personal autonomy within relationships. Communicate your boundaries respectfully and assertively, advocating for your emotional well-being while also respecting the boundaries of others. Healthy boundaries create a sense of safety and respect within relationships, fostering trust and intimacy.

Practice Assertive Communication: Cultivate assertive communication skills that enable you to express your thoughts, feelings, and needs openly and honestly, while also respecting the perspectives and boundaries of others. Avoid passive-aggressive communication or manipulation tactics, as these can undermine trust and create barriers to authentic connection.

Practice Forgiveness and Letting Go: Release grudges, resentments, and past hurts that weigh heavily on your ego and strain relationships. Practice forgiveness, both towards yourself and others, recognizing that holding onto bitterness and resentment only perpetuates suffering and diminishes the potential for healing and growth within relationships.

Prioritize Collaboration and Compromise: Approach conflicts and disagreements within relationships with a spirit of collaboration and compromise. Focus on finding mutually beneficial solutions that honor the needs and preferences of both parties, rather than seeking to assert dominance or control. Collaboration fosters a sense of partnership and teamwork within relationships, creating opportunities for mutual growth and understanding.

Maintaining a healthy balance of ego in relationships requires a commitment to self-awareness, empathy, humility, and collaboration. By cultivating these qualities, individuals can foster deeper levels of intimacy, trust, and connection within their relationships, creating a foundation for lasting love, friendship, and mutual support.

# Chapter 5: Ego and Success

In the realm of human achievement and personal fulfillment, the concept of ego emerges as a compelling force that shapes the pursuit of success and the attainment of goals. Ego, the core of individual identity and self-perception, intertwines with ambition, drive, and aspiration, influencing the pathways individuals navigate in their quest for success. Exploring the dynamic interplay between ego and success unveils a complex tapestry of motivations, challenges, and triumphs that illuminate the human experience.

At its essence, ego represents the lens

through which individuals perceive themselves and their place in the world of achievement. It encompasses a delicate balance of self-confidence, self-esteem, and self-awareness, shaping the narratives individuals construct about their abilities, worth, and potential. Ego drives individuals to set ambitious goals, pursue excellence, and seek validation for their accomplishments, fueling the fires of ambition and innovation that propel them towards success.

Moreover, ego influences the ways in which individuals navigate the challenges and obstacles encountered on the path to success. In the face of setbacks, criticism, and failures, ego can serve as a source of resilience and determination, empowering individuals to persevere in the face of adversity. Conversely, ego can also become a barrier to growth and learning, leading individuals to resist feedback, ignore constructive criticism, or succumb to the pitfalls of arrogance and hubris.

The pursuit of success is often imbued with societal expectations, cultural norms, and personal desires that shape the contours of ambition and achievement. Ego-driven aspirations may be fueled by a desire for recognition, status, or material wealth, reflecting broader values and priorities within society. However, the quest for success can also be driven by a deeper sense of purpose, meaning, and fulfillment that transcends external accolades and validation.

Yet, the pursuit of success is not without its complexities and challenges. Ego-driven motivations may lead individuals to prioritize personal gain over the well-being of others, fostering environments of competition, comparison, and rivalry. Moreover, the relentless pursuit of success can exact a toll on mental health, relationships, and overall well-being, as individuals grapple with the pressures of perfectionism, burnout, and imposter syndrome.

Exploring the relationship between ego and success invites us on a journey of introspection and self-discovery, challenging us to confront the complexities of ambition, achievement, and personal fulfillment. As we navigate the terrain of ego in our pursuit of success, may we cultivate humility, authenticity, and empathy, recognizing that true fulfillment lies not only in external accolades but also in the depth of our relationships, the resilience of our character, and the integrity of our values.

## The connection between ego and ambition

The connection between ego and ambition is an intricate tapestry woven with threads of motivation, drive, and self-perception. Ego, the core of individual identity and self-awareness, intersects with ambition in profound ways, shaping the pathways individuals navigate in their pursuit of goals and aspirations.

At its essence, ego serves as the driving force behind ambition, fueling individuals' desires for achievement, recognition, and success. It encompasses a delicate balance of self-confidence, self-esteem, and self-awareness, influencing the narratives individuals construct about their abilities, worth, and potential. Ego-driven ambitions are often fueled by a desire for validation, status, or external acclaim, reflecting a need to bolster one's sense of self-worth and identity through accomplishments and accolades.

Ego influences the ways in which individuals set and pursue ambitious goals. It provides the impetus for individuals to dream big, take risks, and push beyond their comfort zones in pursuit of excellence. Ego-driven ambitions may be characterized by a relentless pursuit of advancement, growth, and mastery in one's chosen field, as individuals strive to prove their worth and competence to themselves and others.

However, the connection between ego and ambition is not without its complexities and challenges. Ego-driven ambitions can sometimes lead individuals to prioritize personal gain over the well-being of others, fostering environments of competition, comparison, and rivalry. The relentless pursuit of ambition can also exact a toll on mental health, relationships, and overall well-being, as individuals grapple with the pressures of perfectionism, burnout, and imposter syndrome.

Moreover, ego-driven ambitions may be vulnerable to external validation and criticism, as individuals seek affirmation and recognition from others to validate their sense of self-worth and accomplishment. The fear of failure or rejection may loom large in the pursuit of ambitious goals, leading individuals to equate success with self-worth and define their identity solely in terms of external achievements.

Yet, the connection between ego and ambition also holds the potential for growth, resilience, and personal fulfillment. By cultivating self-awareness, humility, and authenticity, individuals can harness the power of ego-driven ambitions to fuel meaningful contributions, purposeful endeavors, and positive impact in the world. Ego-driven ambitions, when tempered with empathy, integrity, and compassion, can become a catalyst for personal growth, creativity, and innovation, fostering environments of collaboration, growth, and shared success.

Exploring the connection between ego and ambition invites us on a journey of introspection and self-discovery, challenging us to confront the complexities of motivation, drive, and self-perception. As we navigate the terrain of ego in our pursuit of ambitious goals, may we cultivate humility, authenticity, and empathy, recognizing that true fulfillment lies not only in external accolades but also in the depth of our relationships, the resilience of our character, and the integrity of our values.

## The dangers of an ego-driven pursuit of success

The dangers of an ego-driven pursuit of

success loom large in the landscape of human achievement, casting shadows of imbalance, disillusionment, and personal disintegration. When ambition becomes entangled with ego, the quest for success can transform from a journey of growth and fulfillment into a perilous pursuit of validation, power, and external acclaim. Understanding the dangers inherent in an ego-driven pursuit of success is essential for safeguarding mental health, well-being, and authentic fulfillment.

One of the primary dangers of an ego-driven pursuit of success lies in the erosion of authenticity and integrity. When individuals prioritize external validation and recognition over personal values and principles, they may compromise their authenticity and ethical standards in the relentless pursuit of success. This can lead to a loss of self-respect, inner conflict, and moral distress as individuals grapple with the disconnect between their actions and their core beliefs.

An ego-driven pursuit of success often breeds a culture of competition, comparison, and rivalry that undermines collaboration, empathy, and mutual support. Individuals may become consumed by a relentless quest for superiority and dominance, viewing others as mere obstacles or competitors to be overcome rather than valued collaborators or allies. This can create toxic work environments, strained relationships, and a sense of isolation as individuals prioritize their own advancement at the expense of meaningful connection and community.

The ego-driven pursuit of success can exact a heavy toll on mental health and emotional well-being. The relentless pressure to achieve, perform, and excel can fuel feelings of inadequacy, anxiety, and burnout as individuals strive to meet unrealistic standards of perfection and success. The fear of failure or rejection may loom large, leading to chronic stress, imposter syndrome, and a pervasive sense of discontentment even in the face of external accomplishments.

In addition, an ego-driven pursuit of success may foster a sense of emptiness and disillusionment as individuals realize that external accolades and achievements do not necessarily equate to true fulfillment and happiness. The pursuit of success becomes an endless treadmill, with each milestone reached merely serving as a stepping stone to the next elusive goal. Without a deeper sense of purpose, meaning, and connection, individuals may find themselves trapped in a cycle of striving and grasping for external validation that ultimately leaves them feeling unfulfilled and spiritually bankrupt.

The dangers of an ego-driven pursuit of success underscore the importance of cultivating humility, authenticity, and inner wisdom in our quest for fulfillment and meaning. By prioritizing values such as integrity, empathy, and genuine connection, individuals can navigate the complexities of ambition and achievement with grace and authenticity, fostering environments of collaboration, growth, and shared success. As we strive for success, may we remember that true fulfillment lies not in the external trappings of success, but in the richness of our relationships, the depth of our character, and the authenticity of our journey.

## Balancing ego and humility in achieving success

Balancing ego and humility in achieving success is a delicate dance that requires self-awareness, introspection, and a deep understanding of one's values and priorities. Ego, the core of individual identity and self-perception, can be a powerful catalyst for ambition, drive, and achievement. However, when left unchecked, ego can also lead to hubris, arrogance, and a disconnect from reality. Humility, on the other hand, offers a grounding force that fosters authenticity, empathy, and genuine connection with others. Balancing these two elements is essential for navigating the complexities of success with grace, integrity, and fulfillment.

At its essence, ego-driven ambition fuels the desire for external validation, recognition, and status. It drives individuals to set ambitious goals, take risks, and push beyond their comfort zones in pursuit of excellence. Ego-driven ambition can be a powerful motivator, providing the impetus for growth, innovation, and personal achievement. However, when ego becomes inflated, individuals may lose sight of their values, integrity, and the well-being of others in the relentless pursuit of success.

Humility, on the other hand, offers a counterbalance to ego-driven ambition. Humility is not about diminishing one's accomplishments or talents but rather about recognizing one's limitations, embracing vulnerability, and acknowledging the contributions of others. Humility fosters a sense of gratitude, empathy, and openness to learning, allowing individuals to approach success with authenticity, integrity, and a willingness to collaborate and grow.

Balancing ego and humility in achieving success requires cultivating self-awareness and emotional intelligence. It involves reflecting on one's motives, values, and aspirations, and discerning whether they are driven by ego-driven ambition or genuine alignment with one's deepest values and purpose. It also involves recognizing the impact of one's actions and decisions on others and fostering empathy, compassion, and a spirit of generosity and service.

Practicing humility in the pursuit of success involves embracing vulnerability, acknowledging mistakes, and learning from failures. It means recognizing that success is not solely a result of individual effort but also of the support, guidance, and contributions of others. It involves celebrating the achievements of others and fostering a culture of collaboration, mutual respect, and shared success.

Ultimately, balancing ego and humility in achieving success requires a commitment to authenticity, integrity, and emotional resilience. It involves embracing the paradox of ambition and humility, recognizing that true success lies not only in external accomplishments but also in the depth of one's relationships, the impact of one's contributions, and the authenticity of one's journey. By cultivating a healthy balance of ego and humility, individuals can navigate the complexities of success with grace, integrity, and a sense of purpose and fulfillment.

# Chapter 6: Ego and Failure

In the intricate tapestry of human experience, the relationship between ego and failure emerges as a profound and often challenging interplay that shapes our perceptions, responses, and growth. Ego, the core of individual identity and self-perception, intersects with failure in myriad ways, influencing how we interpret setbacks, navigate adversity, and define success. Exploring the dynamics of ego and failure unveils a rich tapestry of resilience, vulnerability, and transformation that illuminates the human journey.

At its essence, ego represents the lens through which individuals perceive themselves and their experiences, including failure. It encompasses a delicate balance of self-esteem, self-worth, and self-awareness, shaping the narratives we construct about our abilities, worth, and potential. Ego influences how we internalize failure—whether we see it as a temporary setback, a reflection of our inherent inadequacy, or an opportunity for growth and learning.

Failure, often viewed through the lens of ego, can evoke a range of emotional responses—from shame and embarrassment to frustration and despair. Ego-driven responses to failure may include defensiveness, denial, or blame-shifting as individuals seek to protect their sense of self-worth and preserve their ego identity. However, the ego's resistance to failure can also hinder resilience and growth, trapping individuals in cycles of avoidance, self-doubt, and stagnation.

Yet, the relationship between ego and failure also holds the potential for profound transformation and personal growth. When approached with humility, introspection, and resilience, failure can become a catalyst for self-discovery, innovation, and renewal. By embracing failure as a natural and inevitable part of the human experience, individuals can transcend ego-driven narratives of success and failure, cultivating resilience, adaptability, and a deeper sense of self-awareness.

Moreover, failure challenges the ego's attachment to external validation and societal expectations, inviting individuals to redefine success on their own terms.

Through the process of failure, individuals confront the limitations of ego-driven ambition and perfectionism, embracing vulnerability and authenticity as pathways to true fulfillment and meaning.

Exploring the relationship between ego and failure invites us on a journey of self-discovery, humility, and resilience. As we navigate the complexities of failure, may we cultivate the courage to confront our ego-driven fears and insecurities, embracing setbacks as opportunities for growth, transformation, and deeper connection with ourselves and others. By transcending the limitations of ego and embracing the lessons of failure, we unlock the door to resilience, authenticity, and the boundless potential of the human spirit.

The ego, with its intricate web of self-perception and identity, often acts as a formidable barrier to embracing and learning from failure. Failure, though a natural and inevitable part of the human experience, can evoke a range of ego-driven responses that hinder our ability to grow, adapt, and thrive.

Firstly, the ego is deeply invested in preserving a positive self-image and protecting us from experiences that threaten our sense of worth and competence. When we encounter failure, the ego may perceive it as a direct assault on our identity, triggering feelings of shame, inadequacy, and vulnerability. In an attempt to shield ourselves from these uncomfortable emotions, the ego may resort to defense mechanisms such as denial, blame-shifting, or rationalization, distorting our perceptions and inhibiting our ability to acknowledge and learn from our mistakes.

Moreover, the ego often operates from a fixed mindset, wherein failures are interpreted as evidence of inherent limitations or deficiencies. Individuals with a fixed mindset believe that their abilities and talents are static and immutable, leading them to view failure as a reflection of their inherent inadequacy rather than as an opportunity for growth and learning. This ego-driven mindset can foster feelings of helplessness, resignation, and self-doubt, preventing individuals from embracing challenges and persisting in the face of setbacks.

Furthermore, the ego-driven desire for external validation and approval can exacerbate the fear of failure and perpetuate a relentless pursuit of perfectionism. When our sense of self-worth becomes contingent upon external achievements or accolades, failure is perceived as a threat to our worthiness and acceptance by others. The fear of judgment or rejection may lead individuals to avoid taking risks or pursuing their goals wholeheartedly, sacrificing growth and fulfillment in favor of maintaining a carefully curated image of success.

The ego's influence on our ability to learn from failure lies in its propensity to distort our perceptions, amplify our insecurities, and hinder our capacity for self-reflection and resilience. Overcoming the limitations imposed by the ego requires cultivating self-awareness, embracing vulnerability, and adopting a growth mindset that views failure as a natural and necessary part of the learning process. By recognizing that failure does not define our worth or identity, we can approach setbacks with curiosity, humility, and resilience, harnessing them as opportunities for self-discovery, growth, and transformation. As we navigate the complexities of failure and the ego, may we embrace the lessons they offer and cultivate a deeper understanding of ourselves and the world around us.

Overcoming ego to bounce back from setbacks requires a profound journey of self-discovery, resilience, and humility. Ego, the core of individual identity and self-perception, often serves as a barrier to learning and growth in the face of failure. Its manifestations—pride, defensiveness, and the need for validation—can hinder our ability to navigate setbacks with grace and resilience. However, by cultivating self-awareness, embracing vulnerability, and fostering a growth mindset, individuals can transcend the limitations of ego and emerge stronger and more resilient in the aftermath of failure.

One of the primary ways ego hinders our ability to learn from failure is through defensiveness and denial. When faced with setbacks, our ego may compel us to protect our sense of self-worth and identity by deflecting blame, making excuses, or denying responsibility. This defensive stance prevents us from taking ownership of our mistakes and learning from our failures, perpetuating cycles of stagnation and repeating the same patterns of behavior.

Moreover, ego-driven perfectionism can also impede our ability to bounce back from setbacks. The relentless pursuit of perfection and external validation can create unrealistic expectations and standards that set us up for disappointment and self-doubt when we inevitably fall short. Ego-driven perfectionism stifles creativity, innovation, and resilience, as we become more focused on avoiding failure than embracing the opportunities for growth and learning it presents.

Furthermore, ego can breed a fixed mindset that views failure as a reflection of inherent inadequacy rather than an opportunity for growth and improvement. Individuals with a fixed mindset are more likely to interpret setbacks as evidence of their limited abilities and talents, leading to feelings of helplessness and resignation. This fixed mindset limits our capacity to bounce back from setbacks, as we become mired in self-doubt and defeatism rather than embracing the challenges as opportunities for growth and learning.

To overcome ego and bounce back from setbacks, individuals must cultivate humility, self-awareness, and a growth mindset. Humility allows us to acknowledge our limitations, vulnerabilities, and mistakes without succumbing to shame or defensiveness. It opens the door to self-reflection and introspection, empowering us to take ownership of our failures and learn from our mistakes with courage and resilience.

Additionally, fostering a growth mindset enables us to embrace failure as a natural and inevitable part of the learning process. Rather than viewing setbacks as evidence of our inadequacy, a growth mindset sees them as opportunities for growth, resilience, and personal development. It encourages us to approach challenges with curiosity, perseverance, and a willingness to experiment and adapt in the face of adversity.

Overcoming ego to bounce back from setbacks is a transformative journey that requires courage, humility, and a commitment to lifelong learning and growth. By embracing vulnerability, cultivating self-awareness, and fostering a growth mindset, individuals can transcend the limitations of ego and emerge stronger, wiser, and more resilient in the face of failure. As we navigate the complexities of life's challenges, may we embrace the lessons of failure with humility and grace, recognizing that true resilience lies not in avoiding failure, but in our ability to rise from the ashes and forge a path of courage, authenticity, and growth.

The importance of a growth mindset in dealing with failure cannot be overstated. A growth mindset is a transformative belief system that views failure not as evidence of one's limitations, but as an opportunity for growth, learning, and personal development. Individuals with a growth mindset embrace challenges, persist in the face of setbacks, and see effort as the pathway to mastery and success. In the context of failure, a growth mindset enables individuals to navigate setbacks with resilience, humility, and a sense of possibility, rather than succumbing to defeatism or self-doubt.

One of the key aspects of a growth mindset is the belief that abilities and talents can be developed through dedication, effort, and perseverance. Individuals with a growth mindset understand that intelligence, creativity, and skill are not fixed traits, but rather qualities that can be cultivated and expanded over time. This belief empowers individuals to approach failure as a natural and inevitable part of the learning process, rather than a reflection of their innate abilities or worth.

Moreover, a growth mindset fosters resilience and perseverance in the face of adversity. Rather than viewing setbacks as insurmountable obstacles, individuals with a growth mindset see them as opportunities for growth and learning. They embrace challenges with curiosity

and enthusiasm, recognizing that each
failure brings valuable insights, lessons,
and opportunities for improvement. This
resilience enables individuals to bounce
back from setbacks with grace and
determination, rather than becoming
mired in self-doubt or defeatism.

A growth mindset encourages individuals
to adopt a constructive approach to
failure, focusing on the process of learning
and improvement rather than the
outcome. Rather than dwelling on past
mistakes or shortcomings, individuals with
a growth mindset seek feedback, reflect
on their experiences, and identify
strategies for growth and development.
They view failure as a temporary
setback, not a permanent condition, and
remain committed to their goals and
aspirations despite obstacles or setbacks

along the way.

Importantly, a growth mindset fosters a sense of agency and empowerment in dealing with failure. Individuals with a growth mindset understand that they have the power to shape their own destinies through their attitudes, beliefs, and actions. They take ownership of their failures, recognizing that they have the ability to learn from their mistakes, adapt to new challenges, and ultimately achieve their goals.

The importance of a growth mindset in dealing with failure lies in its transformative power to turn setbacks into opportunities, obstacles into stepping stones, and adversity into growth. By embracing the principles of effort, perseverance, and resilience, individuals with a growth mindset can navigate the complexities of failure with courage, optimism, and a sense of possibility. As we strive for success and fulfillment in life, may we cultivate a growth mindset that enables us to embrace failure as a catalyst for growth, learning, and personal transformation.

# Chapter 7: Ego and Self-Awareness

Ego and self-awareness stand as two fundamental pillars in the realm of human psychology and personal development, shaping our perceptions, behaviors, and interactions with the world. Ego, the core of individual identity and self-perception, encompasses the intricate tapestry of thoughts, emotions, and beliefs that define our sense of self. Self-awareness, on the other hand, represents the capacity to introspectively understand and perceive oneself, including one's strengths, weaknesses, motivations, and emotions.

The dynamic interplay between ego and self-awareness unveils a profound journey of introspection, growth, and transformation that lies at the heart of the human experience. Understanding the nuances of this relationship sheds light on the complexities of identity, authenticity, and personal fulfillment, inviting us to explore the depths of our inner landscapes with curiosity and compassion.

At its essence, ego serves as the lens through which we perceive ourselves and interpret our experiences. It encompasses our beliefs, values, and narratives about who we are, shaping our sense of identity, self-esteem, and self-worth. Ego influences how we navigate the world, influencing our thoughts, emotions, and behaviors as we seek validation, meaning, and purpose in our lives.

Self-awareness, on the other hand, represents the capacity to observe, understand, and reflect upon our thoughts, feelings, and actions with clarity and objectivity. It involves cultivating a deep understanding of our strengths, weaknesses, triggers, and patterns of behavior, allowing us to navigate life with greater insight, authenticity, and resilience.

The relationship between ego and self-awareness is multifaceted and dynamic. On one hand, ego can obscure our self-awareness, leading us to cling to rigid beliefs, defenses, and narratives about ourselves that may limit our growth and potential. Ego-driven defenses such as denial, projection, and rationalization can shield us from confronting uncomfortable truths about ourselves, hindering our capacity for self-awareness and personal growth.

On the other hand, self-awareness can serve as a catalyst for transcending ego-driven patterns and beliefs. Through introspection, mindfulness, and emotional intelligence, we can cultivate a deeper understanding of ourselves, uncovering the layers of conditioning, fears, and insecurities that shape our ego identities. By embracing vulnerability, authenticity, and self-compassion, we can navigate the complexities of ego with grace and wisdom, fostering a greater sense of alignment, fulfillment, and connection with ourselves and others.

The relationship between ego and self-awareness invites us on a transformative journey of self-discovery, growth, and integration. By cultivating self-awareness, we can navigate the complexities of ego with clarity and compassion, fostering greater authenticity, resilience, and fulfillment in our lives. As we embark on this journey of self-exploration, may we embrace the paradox of ego and self-awareness with curiosity and courage, recognizing that true liberation lies in the depths of our own hearts and minds.

## The link between ego and self-awareness

The link between ego and self-awareness forms a foundational aspect of human psychology and personal development, intricately woven into the fabric of our identities, perceptions, and interactions with the world. Ego, the core of individual identity and self-perception, shapes our beliefs, values, and narratives about who we are, influencing our thoughts, emotions, and behaviors. Self-awareness, on the other hand, represents the capacity to introspectively understand and perceive oneself, including one's strengths, weaknesses, motivations, and emotions. Understanding the dynamic interplay between ego and self-awareness unveils a profound journey of introspection, growth, and transformation that lies at the heart of the human experience.

Ego serves as the lens through which we perceive ourselves and interpret our experiences. It encompasses our self-image, self-esteem, and sense of identity, shaping how we navigate the world and interact with others. Our ego identities are constructed from a myriad of factors including societal norms, cultural influences, past experiences, and personal beliefs. They form the basis of our self-concept and inform our thoughts, emotions, and behaviors as we seek validation, meaning, and purpose in our lives.

Self-awareness, meanwhile, involves the ability to observe, understand, and reflect upon our thoughts, feelings, and actions with clarity and objectivity. It requires cultivating a deep understanding of our inner selves, including our strengths, weaknesses, triggers, and patterns of behavior. Self-awareness allows us to navigate life with greater insight, authenticity, and resilience, enabling us to make conscious choices and respond to challenges with wisdom and grace.

The link between ego and self-awareness lies in their mutual influence and interdependence. While ego shapes our perceptions and behaviors, self-awareness provides the foundation for understanding and transcending ego-driven patterns and beliefs. Self-awareness enables us to observe our ego identities with clarity and objectivity, recognizing the ways in which they may be influenced by fears, insecurities, and conditioning. Through introspection and mindfulness, we can uncover the layers of egoic defenses and narratives that shape our self-perception, allowing us to navigate the complexities of ego with greater wisdom and discernment.

Self-awareness fosters a sense of authenticity and alignment with our true selves. By cultivating self-awareness, we can discern between the voice of ego and the voice of our inner wisdom and intuition. we can identify when ego-driven fears and insecurities are influencing our thoughts and behaviors, and consciously choose to respond from a place of clarity, compassion, and authenticity.

The link between ego and self-awareness invites us on a transformative journey of self-discovery and growth. By cultivating self-awareness, we can navigate the complexities of ego with grace and wisdom, fostering greater alignment, fulfillment, and connection with ourselves and others. As we deepen our understanding of the dynamic interplay between ego and self-awareness, we unlock the potential for profound transformation and liberation in our lives.

Cultivating self-awareness and keeping ego in check is a transformative journey that requires commitment, introspection, and a willingness to confront the complexities of our inner selves. By fostering self-awareness and cultivating practices that temper the influence of ego, individuals can navigate life with greater clarity, authenticity, and resilience. Here are some strategies to cultivate self-awareness and keep ego in check:

**Practice Mindfulness:** Mindfulness involves cultivating awareness of the present moment without judgment. By practicing mindfulness meditation, individuals can observe their thoughts, emotions, and bodily sensations with curiosity and acceptance. Mindfulness helps to cultivate self-awareness by allowing individuals to recognize patterns of thought and behavior without becoming overly identified with them.

**Engage in Reflective Practices:** Reflective practices such as journaling, self-inquiry, or introspective writing can deepen self-awareness by providing a space for exploration and reflection. Writing about experiences, emotions, and insights can help individuals gain clarity about their values, beliefs, and motivations, fostering a deeper understanding of themselves and their inner worlds.

**Seek Feedback and Perspective:** Seeking feedback from others can offer valuable insights into our blind spots, biases, and areas for growth. Surrounding ourselves with trusted mentors, friends, or coaches who can offer honest and constructive feedback can help us gain perspective and challenge our ego-driven narratives and defenses.

**Cultivate Empathy and Compassion:** Cultivating empathy and compassion towards ourselves and others fosters a deeper understanding of human nature and interconnectedness. By practicing empathy, individuals can develop a greater capacity to recognize and validate the experiences and perspectives of others, transcending ego-driven tendencies towards judgment and comparison.

**Embrace Vulnerability:** Embracing

vulnerability involves acknowledging and accepting our imperfections, fears, and insecurities with courage and authenticity. By embracing vulnerability, individuals can cultivate greater self-compassion and resilience, allowing them to navigate setbacks and failures with grace and humility.

**Challenge Ego-Driven Beliefs and Assumptions:** Actively challenging ego-driven beliefs and assumptions can help individuals gain clarity and perspective on their thought patterns and behaviors. Questioning assumptions, considering alternative perspectives, and remaining open to new ideas and experiences can help individuals cultivate flexibility and adaptability in their thinking.

**Practice Detachment and Letting Go:**
Practicing detachment involves cultivating a sense of non-attachment to outcomes, identities, and external validation. By letting go of the need to control or define ourselves through external achievements or labels, individuals can cultivate a deeper sense of inner freedom and authenticity.

**Cultivate Humility and Gratitude:**
Cultivating humility and gratitude involves recognizing and appreciating our strengths, accomplishments, and blessings with humility and gratitude. By acknowledging that we are part of something larger than ourselves, individuals can cultivate a sense of humility and interconnectedness that transcends ego-driven tendencies towards arrogance or entitlement.

Cultivating self-awareness and keeping ego in check requires ongoing practice, patience, and self-reflection. By embracing practices that deepen self-awareness and challenge ego-driven tendencies, individuals can navigate life with greater authenticity, resilience, and inner peace. As we cultivate self-awareness and keep ego in check, may we embrace the journey of self-discovery with curiosity, compassion, and an open heart.

## The benefits of a healthy level of self-awareness

The benefits of a healthy level of self-awareness permeate every aspect of our lives, shaping our relationships, decisions, and overall well-being. Self-awareness, the capacity to introspectively understand and perceive oneself, is a foundational aspect of personal growth and development. When cultivated consciously and nurtured over time, a healthy level of self-awareness yields numerous benefits:

**Improved Emotional Regulation:** Self-awareness enhances our ability to recognize and understand our emotions, enabling us to regulate them effectively. By identifying the triggers and patterns of our emotional responses, we can respond to challenging situations with greater composure and resilience.

**Enhanced Self-Understanding:** Self-awareness fosters a deeper understanding of our thoughts, beliefs, values, and motivations. By exploring our inner landscape with curiosity and compassion, we gain insight into our strengths, weaknesses, and areas for growth, allowing us to make informed decisions aligned with our authentic selves.

**Greater Empathy and Compassion:** Cultivating self-awareness fosters empathy and compassion towards ourselves and others. By recognizing our common humanity and shared experiences, we develop a deeper sense of connection and understanding with those around us, fostering empathy, and compassion in our relationships.

**Improved Communication Skills:** Self-awareness enhances our ability to communicate effectively with others. By understanding our communication styles, preferences, and triggers, we can express ourselves authentically and assertively while also listening attentively and empathetically to others' perspectives.

**Enhanced Conflict Resolution:** Self-awareness enables us to navigate conflicts constructively and empathetically. By recognizing our own contributions to conflicts and understanding the perspectives of others, we can engage in productive dialogue, find common ground, and seek mutually beneficial solutions.

**Increased Resilience and Adaptability:** Self-awareness fosters resilience and adaptability in the face of challenges and setbacks. By acknowledging our strengths and limitations, we can approach obstacles with courage and resourcefulness, learning

from failures, and setbacks to emerge
stronger and more resilient.

**Enhanced Decision-Making Abilities:** Self-
awareness enhances our ability to make
informed and values-aligned decisions. By
clarifying our goals, values, and priorities,
we can weigh the potential consequences
of our choices more effectively, making
decisions that resonate with our
authentic selves and long-term
aspirations.

**Improved Leadership Skills:** Self-
awareness is foundational to effective
leadership. Leaders who possess self-
awareness inspire trust, authenticity, and
accountability among their team
members. By understanding their
strengths, weaknesses, and leadership

styles, they can foster a culture of openness, collaboration, and continuous growth within their organizations.

**Better Physical and Mental Health:** Self-awareness contributes to better physical and mental health outcomes. By recognizing the impact of stress, lifestyle choices, and thought patterns on our well-being, we can adopt healthier habits, cope with challenges more effectively, and cultivate a greater sense of overall well-being.

The benefits of a healthy level of self-awareness are far-reaching and profound. By nurturing self-awareness as a lifelong practice, we can cultivate deeper connections, make more informed decisions, and live more authentically aligned lives.

As we continue to explore and deepen our understanding of ourselves, may we embrace the transformative power of self-awareness to enhance our relationships, well-being, and overall quality of life.

# Chapter 8: Ego and Self-Esteem

In the complex landscape of human psychology, the interplay between ego and self-esteem emerges as a profound and multifaceted dynamic that shapes our perceptions, behaviors, and sense of self-worth. Ego, the core of individual identity and self-perception, intertwines with self-esteem, influencing how we perceive ourselves, interact with others, and navigate the world around us. Understanding the intricate relationship between ego and self-esteem unveils a rich tapestry of self-discovery, resilience, and personal growth that lies at the heart of the human experience.

At its essence, ego represents the cognitive and emotional framework through which individuals perceive themselves and interpret their experiences. It encompasses the beliefs, values, and narratives that define our sense of identity and self-worth, shaping how we view ourselves in relation to others and the world. Ego influences our thoughts, emotions, and behaviors, driving our desires for validation, recognition, and acceptance from others.

Self-esteem, on the other hand, reflects the subjective evaluation of one's own worth and value as a person. It encompasses feelings of self-respect, self-acceptance, and self-confidence, influencing how we perceive our abilities, accomplishments, and intrinsic worth. Self-esteem serves as the foundation of our psychological well-being, influencing our mental health, relationships, and overall quality of life.

The relationship between ego and self-esteem is dynamic and multifaceted. While ego influences our self-esteem by shaping our perceptions and beliefs about ourselves, self-esteem, in turn, can impact the strength and stability of our ego identities. Individuals with healthy self-esteem tend to have a more stable and resilient ego, allowing them to navigate challenges and setbacks with confidence and self-assurance.

Conversely, individuals with fragile or low self-esteem may experience greater vulnerability to ego-driven insecurities, self-doubt, and validation-seeking behaviors. Their sense of self-worth may become contingent upon external validation and approval, leading to a perpetual cycle of seeking affirmation and recognition from others to bolster their fragile egos.

Understanding the interplay between ego and self-esteem invites us on a journey of self-discovery, introspection, and personal growth. By cultivating self-awareness and fostering a healthy sense of self-esteem, we can navigate the complexities of ego with grace, authenticity, and resilience. As we explore the intricacies of ego and self-esteem, may we embrace the transformative power of self-discovery and self-acceptance to cultivate deeper connections, inner fulfillment, and authentic expression in our lives.

The impact of ego on self-esteem is profound and multifaceted, shaping how individuals perceive themselves, interact with others, and navigate the complexities of life. Ego, the core of individual identity and self-perception, plays a significant role in influencing the strength, stability, and resilience of self-esteem.

At its core, ego represents the cognitive and emotional framework through which individuals construct their sense of self and navigate the world. It encompasses beliefs, values, and narratives about one's identity, abilities, and intrinsic worth. Ego influences how individuals interpret their experiences, perceive their strengths and weaknesses, and seek validation and recognition from others.

Ego can have both positive and negative impacts on self-esteem, depending on its manifestations and how it is integrated into one's sense of self. A healthy ego, characterized by a balanced sense of self-worth, self-confidence, and self-awareness, can bolster self-esteem and contribute to overall well-being. Individuals with a healthy ego tend to have a stable and resilient sense of self-esteem, grounded in an internal sense of worth and validation.

Conversely, an inflated or fragile ego can undermine self-esteem and lead to a range of maladaptive behaviors and thought patterns. An inflated ego, characterized by grandiosity, arrogance, and a need for superiority, may mask underlying insecurities and vulnerabilities. Individuals with an inflated ego may rely on external validation and accomplishments to bolster their fragile sense of self-esteem, leading to a cycle of validation-seeking behaviors and a diminished capacity for authentic self-acceptance.

Similarly, a fragile ego, characterized by insecurity, self-doubt, and hypersensitivity to criticism, can erode self-esteem and undermine one's sense of worth and value. Individuals with a fragile ego may be highly susceptible to the opinions and judgments of others, interpreting feedback or criticism as a reflection of their inherent inadequacy or unworthiness. This perpetual cycle of self-doubt and validation-seeking behaviors can diminish self-esteem and contribute to feelings of unworthiness and inadequacy.

Ego-driven comparisons and competition can further impact self-esteem, fueling feelings of envy, inadequacy, and resentment towards others. In a culture that often values external achievements and appearances, individuals may measure their self-worth against unrealistic standards and expectations, leading to a distorted sense of self-esteem and a constant striving for validation and approval.

The impact of ego on self-esteem underscores the importance of cultivating self-awareness, authenticity, and resilience in navigating the complexities of ego-driven dynamics. By fostering a healthy sense of self-worth and self-acceptance, individuals can mitigate the negative impact of ego-driven insecurities and cultivate a deeper sense of inner fulfillment and authenticity. As we navigate the intricacies of ego and self-esteem, may we strive to cultivate compassion, authenticity, and resilience in our journey towards self-discovery and personal growth.

## Building a strong sense of self-worth without relying on ego

Building a strong sense of self-worth without relying on ego is a transformative journey of self-discovery, authenticity, and inner fulfillment. While ego-driven narratives often equate self-worth with external validation, achievements, and comparisons, true self-worth emerges from a deep sense of self-acceptance, compassion, and alignment with one's intrinsic value as a human being.

Cultivating a strong sense of self-worth without relying on ego involves embracing authenticity, cultivating self-awareness, and nurturing a compassionate relationship with oneself. Here are key strategies for building a strong sense of self-worth without relying on ego:

**Practice Self-Compassion:** Self-compassion involves extending kindness, understanding, and acceptance towards oneself, especially in moments of struggle or self-doubt. By treating oneself with the same kindness and empathy afforded to others, individuals can cultivate a deeper sense of self-worth rooted in self-acceptance and self-love.

**Cultivate Inner Strengths and Values:** Building a strong sense of self-worth involves recognizing and nurturing inner strengths, values, and qualities that contribute to one's sense of identity and purpose. By identifying core values, passions, and strengths, individuals can cultivate a deeper sense of self-worth grounded in authenticity and alignment with their intrinsic values.

**Set Healthy Boundaries:** Setting healthy boundaries involves honoring one's needs, values, and priorities in relationships and interactions with others. By asserting boundaries and advocating for oneself, individuals can cultivate a sense of self-respect and self-empowerment, contributing to a stronger sense of self-worth independent of external validation or approval.

**Focus on Personal Growth and Development:** Building a strong sense of self-worth involves prioritizing personal growth, learning, and self-improvement. By embracing challenges, seeking new experiences, and expanding one's skills and knowledge, individuals can cultivate a sense of competence, confidence, and self-efficacy that contributes to a stronger sense of self-worth.

**Practice Mindfulness and Self-Reflection:** Mindfulness and self-reflection involve cultivating awareness of one's thoughts, emotions, and behaviors with curiosity and non-judgment. By practicing mindfulness, individuals can observe ego-driven patterns, beliefs, and narratives without becoming overly identified with them, fostering a deeper sense of self-awareness and inner peace.

**Celebrate Authentic Achievements and Milestones:** Celebrating authentic achievements and milestones involves acknowledging and celebrating one's successes, accomplishments, and personal growth, regardless of external validation or recognition. By focusing on intrinsic motivations and personal fulfillment, individuals can cultivate a sense of pride and satisfaction that contributes to a stronger sense of self-worth.

**Seek Support and Connection:** Building a strong sense of self-worth involves seeking support and connection with others who affirm and validate one's intrinsic worth and value as a human being. By surrounding oneself with supportive relationships and communities, individuals can cultivate a sense of belonging and acceptance that bolsters self-worth and resilience.

Building a strong sense of self-worth without relying on ego is a transformative journey of self-discovery, authenticity, and inner fulfillment. By embracing authenticity, cultivating self-awareness, and nurturing self-compassion and self-acceptance, individuals can cultivate a deep sense of intrinsic worth and value that transcends external validation and approval. As we embark on this journey of self-discovery and personal growth, may we embrace the transformative power of self-worth rooted in authenticity, compassion, and inner resilience.

Overcoming insecurities and negative self-talk fueled by the ego is a transformative journey of self-discovery, self-compassion, and empowerment. The ego, with its intricate web of self-perception and identity, often perpetuates patterns of insecurity, self-doubt, and negative self-talk that undermine our sense of worth and well-being. However, by cultivating self-awareness, compassion, and resilience, individuals can transcend ego-driven insecurities and embrace a more authentic and empowered way of being.

One of the first steps in overcoming insecurities fueled by the ego is cultivating self-awareness. This involves becoming attuned to the patterns of thought, emotion, and behavior that contribute to feelings of insecurity and self-doubt. By observing our inner dialogue and recognizing the negative narratives and beliefs perpetuated by the ego, we can begin to disentangle ourselves from their grip and reclaim our sense of agency and self-worth.

Practicing self-compassion is essential in overcoming insecurities fueled by the ego. Self-compassion involves extending kindness, understanding, and acceptance towards ourselves, especially in moments of vulnerability and self-doubt. By treating ourselves with the same empathy and care that we would offer to a friend, we can begin to soften the harsh judgments and criticisms perpetuated by the ego, fostering a deeper sense of self-acceptance and resilience.

Challenging negative self-talk is another crucial aspect of overcoming insecurities fueled by the ego. This involves questioning the validity of self-limiting beliefs and reframing negative narratives with more compassionate and empowering alternatives. By cultivating a growth mindset that views setbacks and challenges as opportunities for learning and growth, we can shift our perspective from one of fear and limitation to one of possibility and resilience.

Building a support network of trusted friends, mentors, or therapists can provide invaluable support and encouragement in overcoming insecurities fueled by the ego. By surrounding ourselves with individuals who affirm and validate our worth and potential, we can cultivate a sense of belonging and connection that counteracts feelings of isolation and inadequacy perpetuated by the ego.

Overcoming insecurities and negative self-talk fueled by the ego requires a commitment to self-awareness, self-compassion, and growth. By cultivating a deeper understanding of ourselves, practicing self-compassion in moments of vulnerability, challenging negative self-talk, and seeking support from others, we can transcend the limitations imposed by the ego and embrace a more authentic and empowered way of being. As we navigate the complexities of our inner world, may we embrace the journey of self-discovery with courage, compassion, and resilience, reclaiming our inherent worth and potential along the way.

# Chapter 9: Ego and Spirituality

Exploring the intricate relationship between ego and spirituality unveils a profound journey of self-discovery, transcendence, and interconnectedness that resonates deeply within the human experience. Ego, the core of individual identity and self-perception, intersects with spirituality, the quest for meaning, purpose, and connection with the divine or higher consciousness. Understanding the dynamic interplay between ego and spirituality invites us to explore the depths of our inner landscapes, confront the illusions of separateness, and awaken to the inherent unity and interconnectedness of all existence.

At its essence, ego represents the

cognitive and emotional framework through which individuals perceive themselves and interpret their experiences. It encompasses beliefs, values, and narratives about identity, worth, and autonomy, shaping how we navigate the world and interact with others. Ego-driven desires for validation, control, and recognition often fuel a sense of separateness and division, leading to suffering, conflict, and disillusionment.

Spirituality, on the other hand, transcends the confines of ego-driven consciousness, offering a pathway to awakening, enlightenment, and liberation from the limitations of the self. Spirituality encompasses a wide spectrum of beliefs, practices, and traditions that seek to connect individuals with a higher power, universal consciousness, or divine presence. It invites us to explore the depths of our inner being, cultivate mindfulness, compassion, and surrender, and awaken to the interconnectedness of all life.

The relationship between ego and spirituality is complex and multifaceted. While ego often seeks to assert its identity and autonomy, spirituality invites individuals to transcend the egoic mind and awaken to the deeper truths of existence. Spiritual practices such as meditation, prayer, yoga, and contemplative inquiry offer pathways to quiet the incessant chatter of the ego, cultivate inner peace, and awaken to the inherent divinity and interconnectedness of all life.

Spirituality offers a transformative

framework for navigating the challenges of ego-driven consciousness, including fear, attachment, and suffering. By cultivating qualities such as compassion, forgiveness, and gratitude, individuals can transcend ego-driven patterns and awaken to the boundless love, wisdom, and grace that permeate the universe.

Exploring the relationship between ego and spirituality invites us on a profound journey of self-discovery, transformation, and awakening. As we navigate the complexities of ego-driven consciousness, may we embrace the wisdom of spirituality to awaken to the deeper truths of existence, cultivate compassion, and foster a sense of unity and interconnectedness with all life. In the depths of our spiritual journey, may we discover the inherent divinity that resides within us and awaken to the timeless wisdom that transcends the limitations of the egoic mind.

## The role of ego in spiritual growth

The role of ego in spiritual growth is a complex and nuanced aspect of the human journey towards awakening and enlightenment. Ego, the core of individual identity and self-perception, plays a significant role in shaping our experiences, beliefs, and perceptions of reality. While often perceived as a barrier to spiritual progress, the ego also serves as a catalyst for self-awareness, transformation, and ultimately, transcendence.

At its core, ego represents the cognitive

and emotional framework through which individuals perceive themselves and interpret their experiences. It encompasses beliefs, values, and narratives about identity, worth, and autonomy, shaping how we navigate the world and interact with others. Ego-driven desires for validation, control, and recognition often fuel a sense of separateness and division, leading to suffering, conflict, and disillusionment.

In the context of spiritual growth, the ego often manifests as the "false self" - the identification with thoughts, emotions, and roles that perpetuate a sense of separation from the divine or higher consciousness. The ego seeks to assert its identity and autonomy, clinging to attachments, beliefs, and desires that reinforce the illusion of separateness from the interconnected web of existence.

Despite its propensity for perpetuating illusions of separateness, the ego also serves as a catalyst for self-awareness and growth on the spiritual path. Through the process of self-inquiry, introspection, and mindfulness, individuals can begin to recognize the patterns, beliefs, and attachments that underlie the egoic mind. By cultivating awareness of ego-driven thoughts, emotions, and behaviors, individuals can begin to disidentify with the false self and awaken to the deeper truths of existence.

The challenges and obstacles presented by the ego offer opportunities for growth, transformation, and ultimately, transcendence. The ego serves as a mirror, reflecting back to us the unconscious patterns and conditioning that limit our capacity for love, compassion, and spiritual realization. By confronting these limitations with courage, humility, and compassion, individuals can begin to unravel the layers of egoic identity and awaken to the deeper dimensions of consciousness.

Spiritual practices such as meditation, mindfulness, and contemplative inquiry offer pathways to quiet the incessant chatter of the ego, cultivate inner peace, and awaken to the inherent divinity and interconnectedness of all life. By cultivating qualities such as compassion, forgiveness, and gratitude, individuals can transcend ego-driven patterns and awaken to the boundless love, wisdom, and grace that permeate the universe.

The role of ego in spiritual growth is multifaceted and paradoxical. While often perceived as a barrier to enlightenment, the ego also serves as a catalyst for self-awareness, transformation, and ultimately, transcendence. By embracing the wisdom of spiritual teachings and practices, individuals can navigate the complexities of ego-driven consciousness, awaken to the deeper truths of existence, and ultimately, realize the profound interconnectedness of all life.

## How ego can hinder our connection to a higher power

The ego, with its intricate web of self-perception and identity, often acts as a significant barrier to establishing and deepening our connection to a higher power or spiritual reality. Rooted in a sense of separateness, control, and attachment to the material world, the ego operates from a limited perspective that obstructs our ability to experience the boundless love, wisdom, and grace of a higher power.

One of the primary ways in which the ego hinders our connection to a higher power is through its relentless pursuit of control and autonomy. The ego thrives on the illusion of self-sufficiency and independence, seeking to assert its identity and will in every aspect of life. This relentless pursuit of control often leads to a sense of resistance or defiance towards the unknown, the mysterious, and the transcendent aspects of existence, limiting our capacity to surrender and trust in a higher power.

The ego's attachment to the material world and identification with transient forms and identities further obstructs our connection to a higher power. The ego tends to equate happiness, fulfillment, and security with external achievements, possessions, and relationships, leading to a perpetual cycle of seeking and grasping for validation and significance in the external world. This preoccupation with the material realm distracts us from the deeper dimensions of existence and inhibits our capacity to attune to the subtle whispers of the divine.

The ego's propensity for judgment, comparison, and division creates barriers to experiencing the interconnectedness and unity that underlies all of creation. When we operate from a place of ego-driven consciousness, we perceive ourselves as separate and distinct from others, fostering feelings of isolation, superiority, or inferiority that obscure our recognition of the inherent divinity that resides within each being.

The ego's insistence on maintaining a fixed and limited sense of self often leads to resistance towards experiences that challenge our existing beliefs, identities, and worldviews. When confronted with experiences of uncertainty, vulnerability, or existential questioning, the ego may respond with defensiveness, skepticism, or denial, preventing us from embracing the transformative power of spiritual growth and awakening.

The ego's influence on our connection to a higher power lies in its tendency to reinforce the illusion of separateness, control, and attachment to the material realm. Overcoming the limitations imposed by the ego requires cultivating qualities such as humility, surrender, and openness to the mysteries of existence. By relinquishing the need for control, releasing attachment to transient forms, and embracing the interconnectedness of all life, we can awaken to the transformative presence of a higher power that resides within and around us, guiding us on our journey of spiritual awakening and evolution.

## Practices for transcending ego and deepening spiritual awareness

Transcending the ego and deepening spiritual awareness is a transformative journey of self-discovery, mindfulness, and inner transformation. While the ego often reinforces a sense of separateness, control, and attachment to the material world, spiritual practices offer pathways to transcend ego-driven consciousness and awaken to the deeper truths of existence. Here are several practices for transcending ego and deepening spiritual awareness:

**Mindfulness Meditation:** Mindfulness meditation involves cultivating present-moment awareness and non-judgmental observation of thoughts, emotions, and sensations. By observing the fluctuations of the mind without attachment or identification, individuals can begin to disentangle themselves from ego-driven patterns and awaken to the spaciousness and stillness of their true nature.

**Self-Inquiry:** Self-inquiry involves questioning the nature of the self and investigating the source of identity and consciousness. By asking questions such as "who am I?" and "what is the nature of awareness?", individuals can pierce through the layers of egoic identification and awaken to the timeless presence of pure awareness that lies beyond the egoic mind.

**Cultivating Presence:** Cultivating presence involves bringing awareness and attention to the present moment, free from the constraints of past conditioning or future projections. By anchoring oneself in the present moment through practices such as breath awareness, body scanning, or mindful movement, individuals can transcend the incessant chatter of the ego and awaken to the richness and vibrancy of life unfolding here and now.

**Practicing Surrender:** Practicing surrender involves relinquishing the need for control and trusting in the unfolding of life's mysteries. By surrendering the ego's relentless pursuit of security and certainty, individuals can open themselves to the flow of grace and wisdom that emanates from a higher power or universal consciousness.

**Cultivating Compassion:** Cultivating compassion involves extending kindness, empathy, and understanding towards oneself and others. By recognizing the inherent interconnectedness of all beings and embracing the universality of suffering, individuals can transcend the ego's tendencies towards judgment, comparison, and division, fostering a sense of unity and compassion that deepens spiritual awareness.

**Engaging in Sacred Rituals:** Engaging in sacred rituals and practices from various spiritual traditions can provide opportunities for connection, reverence, and transcendence. Whether through prayer, chanting, ritualistic ceremony, or sacred pilgrimage, individuals can create sacred spaces and moments that facilitate communion with a higher power and deepen spiritual awareness.

**Studying Spiritual Texts and Teachings:** Studying spiritual texts and teachings from various wisdom traditions can provide insights, inspiration, and guidance on the journey of self-discovery and awakening. By exploring the timeless wisdom contained within sacred texts and teachings, individuals can gain new perspectives, deepen their understanding of spiritual principles, and find resonance with their own inner truth.

**Cultivating Gratitude:** Cultivating gratitude involves recognizing and appreciating the abundance and beauty present in every moment. By shifting focus from scarcity and lack to gratitude and abundance, individuals can transcend the ego's tendencies towards dissatisfaction and craving, awakening to the inherent richness and blessings of life.

Practices for transcending ego and deepening spiritual awareness offer pathways to liberation, awakening, and profound transformation. By cultivating mindfulness, self-inquiry, presence, surrender, compassion, sacred rituals, and gratitude, individuals can transcend ego-driven consciousness and awaken to the timeless wisdom and boundless love that reside within and around them. As we embark on the journey of self-discovery and spiritual awakening, may we embrace these practices with openness, humility, and reverence, trusting in the transformative power of awakening to the deeper truths of existence.

# Chapter 10: Ego and Emotions

Understanding the intricate relationship between ego and emotions unveils a profound exploration of human psychology and the complexities of our inner landscape. Ego, the core of individual identity and self-perception, intertwines with emotions, shaping how we experience and navigate the rich tapestry of human feelings. Exploring the dynamic interplay between ego and emotions invites us to delve into the depths of our consciousness, unravel the complexities of our emotional experiences, and cultivate greater self-awareness and emotional intelligence.

At its essence, ego represents the

cognitive and emotional framework through which individuals perceive themselves and interpret their experiences. It encompasses beliefs, values, and narratives about identity, worth, and autonomy, shaping how we understand and respond to the world around us. Ego-driven desires for validation, control, and recognition often influence the way we experience and express our emotions, shaping our relationships, behaviors, and sense of self.

Emotions, on the other hand, are the complex and multifaceted experiences that color our perceptions and shape our responses to the world. From joy and love to fear and sadness, emotions serve as a powerful lens through which we navigate our experiences, relationships, and inner worlds. Our emotions are deeply intertwined with our sense of identity and self-perception, reflecting our values, beliefs, and underlying desires.

The relationship between ego and emotions is dynamic and multifaceted. While ego influences the way we perceive, interpret, and respond to our emotions, our emotional experiences also have the power to shape our sense of self and identity. Ego-driven desires and attachments often give rise to emotional reactions such as attachment, aversion, and identification, shaping the way we relate to ourselves and others.

The ego can also serve as a barrier to experiencing and processing emotions fully. Ego-driven defenses such as denial, repression, and projection can inhibit our ability to acknowledge and accept the full range of our emotional experiences, leading to inner conflict, disconnection, and suffering.

Exploring the relationship between ego and emotions invites us on a journey of self-discovery, introspection, and emotional healing. By cultivating self-awareness, mindfulness, and compassion, we can begin to unravel the complexities of our emotional experiences, deepen our understanding of ourselves and others, and cultivate greater emotional resilience and well-being. As we navigate the intricacies of ego and emotions, may we embrace the transformative power of self-awareness and compassion to navigate our inner worlds with wisdom, grace, and authenticity.

The influence of ego on our emotions is profound and multifaceted, shaping how we perceive, interpret, and respond to the rich tapestry of human feelings. Ego, the core of individual identity and self-perception, intertwines with emotions in complex ways, influencing the intensity, duration, and expression of our emotional experiences.

One of the primary ways in which ego influences our emotions is through the lens of self-perception and identity. Ego-driven beliefs, narratives, and attachments shape how we view ourselves and interpret our experiences, influencing the emotions that arise in response to different situations. For example, when our ego identifies strongly with success, achievement, or social status, experiences of failure, rejection, or criticism may trigger feelings of inadequacy, shame, or unworthiness.

The ego often seeks to protect and defend its identity, leading to a range of emotional reactions in response to perceived threats or challenges. When our ego feels threatened, whether by external circumstances or internal conflicts, it may respond with emotions such as anger, fear, defensiveness, or resentment as a means of self-preservation and self-protection.

The ego's attachment to outcomes, expectations, and desires can influence the quality and intensity of our emotional experiences. When our ego becomes overly attached to specific outcomes or desires, experiences of disappointment, loss, or uncertainty may evoke intense emotional responses such as sadness, grief, or frustration. The ego's relentless pursuit of pleasure and avoidance of pain can further exacerbate emotional suffering and distress.

Additionally, the ego's tendency towards comparison, judgment, and competition can impact our emotional well-being and interpersonal relationships. When our ego engages in comparison with others, whether in terms of success, appearance, or status, it may fuel feelings of envy, jealousy, or resentment towards those perceived as more successful or fortunate. Similarly, the ego's judgments and criticisms of ourselves and others can contribute to feelings of self-doubt, insecurity, and unworthiness.

The ego's identification with past experiences, traumas, or unresolved conflicts can influence the emotional patterns and triggers that shape our present-day experiences. When our ego becomes entangled in past narratives or wounds, it may perpetuate cycles of fear, anger, or sadness that inhibit our capacity for presence, acceptance, and emotional healing.

The influence of ego on our emotions underscores the interconnectedness of our inner worlds and the intricate interplay between self-perception, identity, and emotional experience. By cultivating self-awareness, mindfulness, and compassion, we can begin to unravel the complexities of ego-driven emotions, cultivate emotional resilience, and embrace the full spectrum of human feelings with openness, authenticity, and grace. As we navigate the intricacies of ego and emotions, may we embrace the transformative power of self-discovery and emotional awareness to navigate our inner landscapes with wisdom, compassion, and resilience.

Managing ego-driven emotions such as anger, jealousy, and pride

Managing ego-driven emotions, such as anger, jealousy, and pride, is a crucial aspect of emotional intelligence and personal growth. These emotions, when fueled by the ego, can lead to destructive behaviors, strained relationships, and hindered well-being. By adopting mindful practices and strategies, individuals can learn to navigate and transform these ego-driven emotions into opportunities for self-awareness, growth, and positive change.

**Cultivating Self-Awareness:** Begin by cultivating self-awareness to recognize when ego-driven emotions arise. Pay attention to the physical sensations, thoughts, and behaviors associated with anger, jealousy, or pride. Mindful observation allows you to step back and objectively observe your emotional responses.

**Mindful Breathing and Grounding Techniques:** When strong emotions surface, practice mindful breathing or grounding techniques. Deep, intentional breaths can help calm the nervous system and create space between the triggering event and your reaction. Grounding techniques, such as focusing on the senses or connecting with the present moment, can bring you back to a state of balance.

**Reflective Practices:** Engage in reflective practices such as journaling to explore the underlying causes of ego-driven emotions. Ask yourself why a particular situation triggered such a response and whether there are patterns or beliefs at play. Reflecting on the root causes can unveil insights and pave the way for emotional healing.

**Empathy and Perspective-Taking:** Practice empathy by considering the perspectives of others involved. Understanding that everyone has their own struggles, insecurities, and challenges can foster compassion. This shift in perspective can mitigate ego-driven emotions by promoting understanding and connection.

**Emotional Regulation Techniques:** Develop emotional regulation techniques to manage the intensity of ego-driven emotions. This may include finding healthy outlets for expression, such as exercise or creative activities. Learning to express emotions in constructive ways prevents them from escalating into destructive behaviors.

**Humility and Humbleness:** Cultivate humility and humbleness to counteract the effects of ego-driven pride. Recognize that everyone is on their unique journey, and acknowledging your imperfections and mistakes fosters personal growth. Humility opens the door to authentic connections and collaborative relationships.

**Practice Gratitude:**  Shift focus from what you lack to what you appreciate. Practicing gratitude can counteract jealousy and pride by fostering a positive mindset. Recognizing and appreciating the positives in your life helps create a sense of abundance and contentment.

**Setting Healthy Boundaries:** Establish and communicate healthy boundaries to prevent situations that trigger ego-driven emotions. Setting clear expectations for yourself and others creates a supportive environment, reducing the likelihood of conflict.

**Seeking Support:** Reach out to trusted friends, mentors, or mental health professionals for support and guidance. Sharing your experiences with others can provide valuable insights, alternative perspectives, and emotional support.

**Continuous Learning and Growth:** Embrace a mindset of continuous learning and growth. Ego-driven emotions often arise from a fixed mindset or resistance to change. Embracing challenges as opportunities for learning and personal development can transform negative emotions into catalysts for positive change.

Managing ego-driven emotions involves a combination of self-awareness, mindfulness, empathy, and intentional practices. By approaching these emotions with curiosity and a commitment to personal growth, individuals can transform challenging emotional experiences into opportunities for greater self-understanding and emotional well-being. As we navigate the complexities of ego-driven emotions, may we cultivate resilience, compassion, and a deep sense of authenticity on our journey towards emotional mastery.

## Cultivating emotional intelligence to keep ego in check

Cultivating emotional intelligence is a powerful means of keeping the ego in check, fostering greater self-awareness, empathy, and resilience in navigating the complexities of human emotions and relationships. Emotional intelligence encompasses the ability to recognize, understand, and manage both our own emotions and those of others, enabling us to respond to life's challenges with wisdom, grace, and authenticity.

**Self-Awareness:** Self-awareness forms the foundation of emotional intelligence, allowing individuals to recognize and understand their own emotions, triggers, and patterns of behavior. By cultivating mindfulness and introspection, individuals can develop a deeper understanding of how the ego influences their thoughts, emotions, and actions, empowering them to make conscious choices and responses in the face of ego-driven impulses.

**Self-Regulation:** Self-regulation involves the ability to manage and regulate one's emotions, impulses, and reactions in various situations. By developing emotional resilience and impulse control, individuals can prevent ego-driven emotions such as anger, jealousy, and pride from escalating into destructive behaviors or conflicts. Self-regulation also involves setting healthy boundaries, practicing assertiveness, and seeking support when needed to navigate challenging emotions effectively.

**Empathy:** Empathy is the capacity to understand and share the feelings and perspectives of others, fostering deeper connections and understanding in relationships. By cultivating empathy, individuals can transcend the limitations of ego-driven perceptions and judgments, fostering greater compassion, understanding, and harmony in their interactions with others. Empathy allows individuals to recognize the humanity and vulnerability of others, reducing the tendency towards ego-driven behaviors such as judgment, criticism, or defensiveness.

**Social Skills:** Social skills encompass the ability to effectively navigate social interactions, communicate assertively, and build positive relationships with others. By honing interpersonal skills such as active listening, conflict resolution, and collaboration, individuals can foster healthy and authentic connections that transcend ego-driven dynamics. Social skills also involve the ability to express emotions constructively, assert boundaries, and resolve conflicts with empathy and respect.

**Adaptability:** Adaptability involves the capacity to adapt and thrive in the face of change, uncertainty, and adversity. By embracing flexibility and openness to new experiences, individuals can navigate ego-driven attachments and expectations with greater ease and resilience. Cultivating adaptability allows individuals to relinquish the need for control and certainty, embracing the inherent fluidity and impermanence of life with grace and resilience.

**Mindful Communication:** Mindful communication involves expressing oneself authentically and compassionately while also listening deeply to others with empathy and openness. By practicing mindful communication, individuals can transcend ego-driven tendencies such as defensiveness, judgment, and manipulation, fostering greater clarity, understanding, and connection in their interactions. Mindful communication allows individuals to express their needs, feelings, and boundaries assertively while also honoring the perspectives and experiences of others.

Cultivating emotional intelligence is essential for keeping the ego in check and fostering greater harmony, authenticity, and resilience in our lives and relationships. By developing self-awareness, self-regulation, empathy, social skills, adaptability, and mindful communication, individuals can navigate ego-driven emotions and dynamics with wisdom, grace, and authenticity, fostering greater well-being and fulfillment in their lives. As we cultivate emotional intelligence, may we embrace the transformative power of self-awareness and compassion to navigate the complexities of human emotions and relationships with wisdom, grace, and authenticity.

# Chapter 11: Ego and Identity

Ego and identity stand as pillars in the complex architecture of human psychology and self-perception. Rooted in the depths of consciousness, ego and identity shape how individuals perceive themselves, relate to others, and navigate the world around them. This intricate interplay between ego and identity lies at the heart of human experience, influencing thoughts, emotions, and behaviors in profound ways.

At its core, ego represents the center of individual identity and self-perception. It encompasses the beliefs, values, and narratives that individuals construct to define themselves and make sense of their experiences. Ego serves as a lens through which individuals interpret the world, shaping perceptions of self-worth, autonomy, and belonging. From the ego's perspective, identity is a tapestry woven from memories, desires, and societal influences, reflecting a sense of individuality and separateness from others.

Identity, on the other hand, encompasses the multifaceted aspects of self that contribute to a sense of continuity and coherence over time. It encompasses cultural, social, and personal dimensions that shape how individuals perceive themselves in relation to others and the world. Identity is fluid and dynamic, evolving in response to life experiences, relationships, and cultural influences. It encompasses aspects such as ethnicity, gender, religion, occupation, and personal values, contributing to a sense of belonging and connection within social and cultural contexts.

The relationship between ego and identity is complex and nuanced, with each influencing and shaping the other in profound ways. Ego provides a sense of continuity and coherence to the ever-changing landscape of identity, anchoring individuals in a sense of self amidst the flux of life's experiences. Identity, in turn, informs the narratives and beliefs that comprise ego, shaping how individuals perceive themselves and their place in the world.

Exploring the dynamics of ego and identity

invites us to delve into the depths of human consciousness and self-perception. It prompts questions about the nature of selfhood, the construction of identity, and the ways in which ego influences perceptions of reality and relationships with others. By unraveling the complexities of ego and identity, individuals can cultivate greater self-awareness, authenticity, and resilience in navigating the intricacies of human existence.

The exploration of ego and identity offers a gateway to understanding the complexities of human psychology and self-perception. It invites individuals to delve into the depths of consciousness, unravel the intricacies of identity, and cultivate greater self-awareness and authenticity in their journey towards wholeness and fulfillment. As we navigate the terrain of ego and identity, may we embrace the transformative power of self-discovery and self-expression, forging deeper connections with ourselves and the world around us.

## The relationship between ego and identity

The relationship between ego and identity is intricate and profound, forming the cornerstone of human psychology and self-perception. Ego, often understood as the center of individual consciousness, and identity, the multifaceted sense of self, intertwine in complex ways, influencing how individuals perceive themselves, relate to others, and navigate the world around them.

Ego, in its essence, serves as the lens through which individuals perceive and interpret their experiences. It encompasses the beliefs, values, and narratives that individuals construct to define themselves and make sense of the world. Ego anchors individuals in a sense of individuality and separateness, providing a framework for understanding one's place in the world and relationships with others. It shapes perceptions of self-worth, autonomy, and identity, influencing thoughts, emotions, and behaviors in profound ways.

Identity, on the other hand, encompasses the various dimensions of self that contribute to a sense of continuity and coherence over time. It encompasses cultural, social, and personal aspects that shape how individuals perceive themselves in relation to others and the world. Identity is fluid and dynamic, evolving in response to life experiences, relationships, and cultural influences. It encompasses aspects such as ethnicity, gender, religion, occupation, and personal values, contributing to a sense of belonging and connection within social and cultural contexts.

The relationship between ego and identity is symbiotic, with each influencing and shaping the other in profound ways. Ego provides a sense of continuity and coherence to the ever-changing landscape of identity, anchoring individuals in a sense of self amidst the flux of life's experiences. It serves as the repository of memories, desires, and beliefs that inform one's understanding of oneself and the world. Identity, in turn, informs the narratives and beliefs that comprise ego, shaping how individuals perceive themselves and their place in the world.

However, the relationship between ego and identity is not static but dynamic, evolving over time in response to internal and external influences. Individuals may undergo periods of identity exploration and transformation, challenging and reshaping the narratives and beliefs that comprise ego. Life experiences, relationships, and cultural influences also shape and inform the construction of identity, contributing to its fluidity and complexity.

Exploring the relationship between ego and identity invites individuals to delve into the depths of human consciousness and self-perception. It prompts questions about the nature of selfhood, the construction of identity, and the ways in which ego influences perceptions of reality and relationships with others. By unraveling the complexities of ego and identity, individuals can cultivate greater self-awareness, authenticity, and resilience in navigating the intricacies of human existence. As we navigate the terrain of ego and identity, may we embrace the transformative power of self-discovery and self-expression, forging deeper connections with ourselves and the world around us.

## How ego can limit our sense of self and potential

The ego, while serving as a crucial aspect of human consciousness, can also become a limiting force that constrains our sense of self and potential. Rooted in the need for identity and self-preservation, the ego operates from a perspective of separateness and self-interest, often leading to narrow perceptions and self-imposed limitations. Here's how the ego can limit our sense of self and potential:

**Attachment to Identity:** The ego thrives on maintaining a fixed sense of identity based on past experiences, beliefs, and social roles. This attachment to identity can prevent individuals from exploring new aspects of themselves or embracing change and growth. When the ego becomes overly invested in preserving a particular identity, individuals may resist opportunities for self-exploration and personal development, thus limiting their potential for growth and fulfillment.

**Fear of Failure and Rejection:** The ego is deeply invested in protecting the self-image and avoiding experiences that threaten its sense of worth and competence. Fear of failure and rejection can prevent individuals from taking risks, pursuing their passions, or stepping outside of their comfort zones. When the ego dictates decision-making based on a fear of failure or judgment from others, individuals may forego opportunities for growth and self-expression, thus limiting their potential for success and fulfillment.

**Comparison and Competition:** The ego often operates from a mindset of comparison and competition, constantly measuring oneself against others and seeking validation and superiority. This mindset fosters feelings of inadequacy, envy, and resentment towards those perceived as more successful or accomplished. When individuals define their self-worth and potential based on external achievements or comparisons with others, they limit their ability to cultivate authentic self-esteem and pursue paths aligned with their true passions and values.

**Rigid Belief Systems:** The ego is prone to adopting rigid belief systems and ideologies that reinforce its sense of identity and worldview. These belief systems may be influenced by cultural, societal, or familial conditioning and can act as barriers to open-mindedness and growth. When individuals cling to fixed beliefs and perspectives, they may close themselves off to new ideas, experiences, and possibilities, thus limiting their potential for learning and self-discovery.

**Resistance to Change:** The ego often resists change and uncertainty, preferring the safety and familiarity of the status quo. This resistance to change can manifest as reluctance to step outside of one's comfort zone, explore new opportunities, or adapt to evolving circumstances. When individuals allow the ego's resistance to dictate their actions, they may remain stagnant and unfulfilled, missing out on opportunities for personal and professional growth.

The ego can limit our sense of self and potential by perpetuating attachment to identity, fear of failure, comparison and competition, rigid belief systems, and resistance to change. Overcoming these limitations requires cultivating self-awareness, courage, and a willingness to challenge the ego's grip on our perceptions and behaviors. By embracing vulnerability, embracing uncertainty, and cultivating a growth mindset, individuals can transcend the constraints of the ego and unlock their full potential for self-discovery, fulfillment, and contribution to the world.



Letting go of ego is a profound journey of self-discovery and transformation, opening the door to uncovering our true identity and purpose in life. Ego, with its layers of self-perception, attachment, and fear, often obscures the deeper truths of our existence and prevents us from aligning with our authentic selves. By releasing the grip of ego, individuals can embark on a path of self-discovery, liberation, and alignment with their higher purpose.

**Unveiling the True Self:** Letting go of ego involves peeling away the layers of conditioning, beliefs, and identities that have accumulated over time. It requires courage and introspection to question the narratives and roles that ego has constructed, allowing space for the emergence of the true self beneath the surface. As individuals shed the masks of ego, they come into closer contact with their authentic essence, discovering the inherent wisdom, love, and wholeness that reside within.

**Releasing Attachments and Expectations:** Ego thrives on attachments to outcomes, identities, and external validations. Letting go of ego entails releasing these attachments and expectations, relinquishing the need for approval or recognition from others. By detaching from external markers of success or identity, individuals free themselves from the burden of striving and seeking fulfillment outside of themselves. Instead, they learn to find contentment and meaning from within, rooted in their inherent worth and connection to the present moment.

**Embracing Vulnerability and Impermanence:** Letting go of ego requires embracing vulnerability and accepting the impermanence of life. Ego often seeks to shield us from discomfort and uncertainty, leading to resistance and avoidance of experiences that challenge our sense of control or security. However, by leaning into vulnerability and embracing the ebb and flow of life, individuals cultivate resilience and openness to the richness of human experience. They learn to embrace the beauty of impermanence, finding freedom and growth in the midst of life's inevitable changes.

**Aligning with Higher Purpose:** Letting go of ego allows individuals to align with their higher purpose and contribute meaningfully to the world. As ego dissolves, individuals gain clarity and insight into their unique gifts, passions, and values. They recognize that their true purpose extends beyond personal gain or recognition, encompassing a deeper calling to serve others and contribute to the greater good. By aligning with their higher purpose, individuals find fulfillment and joy in living authentically and making a positive impact on the world around them.

**Cultivating Compassion and Connection:**
Letting go of ego fosters compassion and connection with others, transcending the barriers of separation and judgment that ego creates. As individuals recognize the shared humanity and interconnectedness of all beings, they cultivate empathy, kindness, and understanding in their relationships. They approach interactions with humility and curiosity, recognizing that each person carries their own struggles, fears, and aspirations. Through compassion and connection, individuals forge deeper bonds and create spaces of healing and transformation for themselves and others.

Letting go of ego is a transformative journey that invites individuals to rediscover their true identity and purpose in life. By releasing attachments, embracing vulnerability, aligning with higher purpose, and cultivating compassion, individuals embark on a path of self-discovery, liberation, and authentic living. As they let go of ego, they awaken to the boundless potential and beauty of their true selves, embracing the richness of life with open hearts and minds.

# Chapter 12: Ego and Comparison

In the intricate tapestry of human psychology, ego and comparison stand as intertwined threads, shaping how individuals perceive themselves, relate to others, and navigate the complexities of life. Ego, the intricate web of self-perception and identity, often intertwines with comparison, fueling a perpetual cycle of measuring oneself against others and seeking validation, superiority, or belonging.

Comparison, rooted in the ego's need for validation and recognition, manifests in various forms throughout human experience. From the subtle comparisons of achievements and appearances to the pervasive comparisons fostered by social media and societal standards, the impulse to measure oneself against others is ingrained in the fabric of human consciousness.

At its core, comparison reflects the ego's relentless pursuit of self-definition and validation. It often emerges from a sense of inadequacy, insecurity, or fear of judgment, prompting individuals to seek external benchmarks for self-worth and validation. Whether it's comparing one's achievements, possessions, relationships, or physical appearance, comparison becomes a lens through which individuals evaluate their own value and significance in relation to others.

The pursuit of comparison is fraught with pitfalls and illusions. While it may provide temporary reassurance or validation, comparison often leads to feelings of inadequacy, envy, and resentment towards those perceived as more successful or fortunate. The relentless cycle of comparison perpetuates a sense of separateness and competition, undermining genuine connections and fostering a culture of comparison and competition.

Comparison obscures the inherent worth and uniqueness of each individual, reducing complex human experiences and identities to superficial markers of success or failure. It diminishes the richness of human diversity and potential, reinforcing narrow standards and expectations that limit individual expression and fulfillment.

Exploring the dynamics of ego and comparison invites individuals to delve into the depths of human consciousness and self-perception. It prompts questions about the nature of identity, self-worth, and authenticity in an interconnected world shaped by comparison and competition. By unraveling the complexities of ego and comparison, individuals can cultivate greater self-awareness, compassion, and resilience in navigating the intricacies of human existence.

The exploration of ego and comparison offers a gateway to understanding the complexities of human psychology and self-perception. It invites individuals to transcend the limitations of comparison and cultivate a deeper sense of self-worth, authenticity, and connection with themselves and others. As we navigate the terrain of ego and comparison, may we embrace the transformative power of self-discovery and self-acceptance, forging deeper connections with ourselves and the world around us.



The destructive nature of ego-driven comparison permeates through various aspects of human experience, fostering a toxic cycle of judgment, inadequacy, and resentment that undermines individual well-being and societal harmony. Rooted in the ego's insatiable need for validation and superiority, ego-driven comparison not only erodes self-esteem but also perpetuates harmful dynamics of competition, envy, and disconnection.

**Undermining Self-Worth:** Ego-driven comparison thrives on the premise of evaluating one's worth and significance based on external standards and benchmarks. Individuals often measure their achievements, possessions, or relationships against those of others, leading to a relentless pursuit of validation and recognition. However, this constant comparison erodes self-worth by reinforcing feelings of inadequacy and unworthiness when individuals perceive themselves as falling short of societal or peer expectations.

**Fueling Envy and Resentment:** Comparison breeds envy and resentment towards those perceived as more successful, attractive, or fortunate. The relentless exposure to idealized images and lifestyles through social media and mainstream media exacerbates feelings of envy and inadequacy, fueling a perpetual cycle of discontentment and comparison. Instead of celebrating the success and achievements of others, individuals may harbor feelings of resentment and hostility, leading to fractured relationships and social dynamics.

**Creating a Culture of Competition:** Ego-driven comparison perpetuates a culture of competition and comparison, where individuals constantly vie for recognition and validation at the expense of genuine connection and collaboration. The pursuit of external validation and superiority undermines the spirit of cooperation and mutual support, fostering an environment where individuals prioritize individual success over collective well-being.

**Diminishing Authenticity and Fulfillment:** Comparison obscures the authenticity and uniqueness of each individual, reducing complex human experiences and identities to superficial markers of success or failure. The relentless pursuit of external validation and conformity stifles individual expression and fulfillment, leading to a sense of disconnection and alienation from one's true self. Instead of embracing authenticity and self-discovery, individuals may succumb to societal pressures and expectations, sacrificing personal fulfillment for external validation.

**Perpetuating Inequality and Injustice:** Ego-driven comparison perpetuates inequality and injustice by reinforcing narrow standards of success and worthiness that marginalize certain individuals or groups. The relentless pursuit of external validation and superiority perpetuates systemic inequalities based on factors such as race, gender, socioeconomic status, and physical appearance, further exacerbating disparities in opportunities and access to resources.

The destructive nature of ego-driven comparison undermines individual well-being, fosters toxic social dynamics, and perpetuates systemic inequalities. By unraveling the complexities of ego-driven comparison, individuals can cultivate greater self-awareness, compassion, and resilience, forging deeper connections with themselves and others. As we navigate the terrain of ego and comparison, may we embrace the transformative power of self-acceptance, empathy, and authenticity, fostering a culture of inclusivity, connection, and mutual respect.

Overcoming the incessant need to compare ourselves to others is a transformative journey of self-awareness, acceptance, and growth. In a world inundated with social media and societal pressures, the urge to measure our worth and success against others can be relentless. However, by cultivating mindfulness, self-compassion, and a deeper sense of self-worth, individuals can break free from the destructive cycle of comparison and embrace a path of authenticity and fulfillment.

**Cultivating Self-Awareness:** The first step in overcoming the need to compare ourselves to others is cultivating self-awareness. This involves recognizing the triggers and underlying beliefs that drive our tendency to compare. By observing our thoughts and emotions without judgment, we can gain insight into the root causes of comparison and begin to challenge the validity of these beliefs.

**Practicing Gratitude:** Gratitude is a powerful antidote to comparison, shifting our focus from what we lack to what we already have. By cultivating a daily practice of gratitude, we train our minds to appreciate the abundance and blessings present in our lives. This helps to counteract feelings of envy and inadequacy, fostering a sense of contentment and fulfillment.

**Fostering Self-Compassion:** Self-compassion is essential in overcoming the need for comparison, as it involves treating ourselves with kindness and understanding, especially in moments of struggle or perceived failure. Instead of harsh self-criticism, we can learn to embrace our imperfections and vulnerabilities with compassion and empathy, recognizing that we are worthy of love and acceptance just as we are.

**Setting Meaningful Goals:** Rather than comparing ourselves to others based on external markers of success, we can focus on setting goals that are meaningful and aligned with our values and aspirations. By clarifying our priorities and defining success on our own terms, we can cultivate a sense of purpose and direction that transcends superficial comparisons.

**Limiting Exposure to Triggers:** In today's digital age, it's easy to get caught up in the endless cycle of comparison fueled by social media and online platforms. To mitigate the impact of these triggers, we can take proactive steps to limit our exposure to comparison-inducing content and cultivate a more intentional relationship with technology. This might involve setting boundaries around social media usage, curating our online environments to reflect positive and uplifting content, and prioritizing real-life connections and experiences.

**Celebrating Others' Successes:** Instead of viewing others' successes as threats to our own, we can learn to celebrate and support their achievements with genuine joy and admiration. Cultivating a mindset of abundance and collaboration allows us to recognize that someone else's success does not diminish our own potential or worth. By fostering a sense of interconnectedness and mutual support, we create a culture of empowerment and upliftment where everyone can thrive.

Overcoming the need to constantly compare ourselves to others requires a commitment to self-awareness, self-compassion, and authenticity. By embracing our unique strengths, values, and journeys, we can cultivate a deep sense of self-worth and fulfillment that transcends the illusion of comparison. As we embark on this transformative journey, may we embrace the beauty of our individuality and celebrate the richness of human diversity with open hearts and minds.

Embracing our unique journey and strengths without ego is a profound practice of self-discovery, humility, and authenticity. It involves recognizing and celebrating the inherent worth and beauty of our individual experiences, talents, and contributions without succumbing to the need for external validation or comparison. By cultivating a mindset of gratitude, acceptance, and interconnectedness, individuals can embrace their unique journey and strengths with grace and authenticity, fostering a deep sense of fulfillment and purpose.

**Cultivating Gratitude:** Embracing our

unique journey begins with cultivating gratitude for the experiences, challenges, and blessings that have shaped us into who we are today. By acknowledging the richness and complexity of our individual paths, we can develop a deep sense of appreciation for the opportunities and lessons that each moment presents. Cultivating gratitude allows us to shift our focus from what we lack to what we already have, fostering a sense of abundance and contentment in the present moment.

**Honoring Our Authenticity:** Embracing our unique strengths involves honoring our authenticity and staying true to ourselves in the face of societal expectations and pressures. It requires courage to embrace our individuality and express ourselves authentically, even when it means going against the grain or challenging prevailing norms. By embracing our authenticity, we cultivate a sense of integrity and wholeness that empowers us to live in alignment with our values and aspirations.

**Fostering Humility:** Embracing our unique journey without ego requires fostering humility and openness to learning and growth. Humility involves recognizing that we are all works in progress, imperfect beings on a journey of self-discovery and evolution. By embracing humility, we remain open to new perspectives, experiences, and possibilities, allowing us to expand our understanding of ourselves and the world around us.

**Celebrating Diversity and Interconnectedness:** Embracing our unique journey involves celebrating the diversity and interconnectedness of the human experience. Each individual brings a unique set of talents, perspectives, and experiences to the tapestry of humanity, enriching the collective whole with their unique contributions. By celebrating diversity and recognizing the interconnectedness of all beings, we cultivate a sense of empathy, compassion, and appreciation for the richness of human experience.

**Cultivating Inner Strength and Resilience:** Embracing our unique strengths involves cultivating inner strength and resilience to navigate life's challenges and adversities. It requires trusting in our inherent worth and capabilities, even in the face of uncertainty or setbacks. By cultivating resilience, we develop the courage and resilience to persevere in the pursuit of our goals and aspirations, embracing challenges as opportunities for growth and self-discovery.

**Practicing Self-Compassion and Self-Care:** Embracing our unique journey requires practicing self-compassion and self-care to nurture our physical, emotional, and spiritual well-being. Self-compassion involves treating ourselves with kindness and understanding, especially in moments of struggle or self-doubt. By prioritizing self-care and nourishing our mind, body, and spirit, we create a foundation of resilience and well-being that allows us to thrive in all aspects of our lives.

Embracing our unique journey and strengths without ego is a

transformative practice of self-discovery, authenticity, and humility. By cultivating gratitude, honoring our authenticity, fostering humility, celebrating diversity, cultivating inner strength, and practicing self-compassion, we can embrace our unique journey with grace and authenticity, fostering a deep sense of fulfillment and purpose in our lives. As we embrace the beauty of our individuality and celebrate the richness of human diversity, may we cultivate a culture of acceptance, compassion, and interconnectedness that honors the inherent worth and dignity of every being.

# Chapter 13: Ego and Mindfulness

In the realm of human consciousness, the interplay between ego and mindfulness unfolds as a profound exploration of self-awareness, presence, and inner transformation. Ego, the complex web of self-perception and identity, often shapes our thoughts, emotions, and behaviors, fueling a perpetual cycle of attachment, comparison, and resistance. Mindfulness, on the other hand, offers a path to liberation from the confines of ego, inviting individuals to cultivate a deep sense of presence, acceptance, and clarity in the present moment.

At its core, ego operates from a

perspective of separation and identification with the mind's narratives and perceptions. It thrives on the incessant chatter of thoughts, judgments, and desires, leading individuals to become entangled in a web of attachment and aversion. Ego-driven patterns of thinking and behavior often perpetuate feelings of dissatisfaction, anxiety, and disconnection from the present moment, hindering our ability to experience true peace and fulfillment.

Mindfulness, rooted in ancient contemplative traditions and modern psychological insights, offers a transformative antidote to the tyranny of ego. It involves cultivating a non-judgmental awareness of our thoughts, emotions, and sensations as they arise in the present moment. By practicing mindfulness, individuals develop the capacity to observe the fluctuations of the mind without becoming ensnared in its dramas and illusions. They learn to embrace each moment with openness, curiosity, and acceptance, fostering a deep sense of connection with themselves and the world around them.

The relationship between ego and mindfulness is one of profound inquiry and discovery. Mindfulness invites individuals to investigate the nature of their own consciousness, illuminating the conditioned patterns and beliefs that underlie the ego's grip on perception and identity. Through the practice of mindfulness, individuals learn to cultivate a spacious awareness that transcends the limitations of ego, allowing them to experience life with greater clarity, compassion, and equanimity.

The exploration of ego and mindfulness offers a pathway to inner freedom and awakening. It invites individuals to cultivate a deep sense of self-awareness and presence, liberating themselves from the confines of ego-driven patterns of thinking and behavior. As we embark on this journey of self-discovery and transformation, may we embrace the transformative power of mindfulness to awaken to the fullness of our being, and to live with greater joy, peace, and authenticity.

The connection between ego and the mind delves into the intricate workings of human consciousness, perception, and self-awareness. Ego, often regarded as the center of individual identity and self-perception, is deeply intertwined with the functioning of the mind, influencing thoughts, emotions, and behaviors in profound ways.

At its core, the ego represents the mental construct through which individuals perceive themselves as separate entities, distinct from others and the world around them. It encompasses the beliefs, values, and narratives that individuals construct to define themselves and make sense of their experiences. The ego serves as a filter through which sensory information is processed, shaping perceptions of self-worth, autonomy, and identity.

The mind, on the other hand, encompasses the broader landscape of cognitive processes, including perception, memory, reasoning, and emotion. It serves as the seat of consciousness, housing the myriad thoughts, sensations, and perceptions that constitute the human experience. The mind operates on multiple levels, ranging from conscious awareness to subconscious processes that shape behavior and perception.

The connection between ego and the mind lies at the heart of human psychology and self-awareness. The ego influences the way individuals interpret and respond to stimuli from the external environment, filtering sensory information through the lens of personal identity and self-interest. It shapes cognitive processes such as attention, memory, and decision-making, influencing the way individuals perceive themselves and their place in the world.

Moreover, the ego is closely linked to the formation of beliefs, attitudes, and self-concepts that influence behavior and emotional responses. It often manifests in patterns of thought characterized by self-referential processing, rumination, and attachment to outcomes and identities. The ego's influence extends beyond conscious awareness, permeating subconscious processes and influencing behavior in subtle ways.

The connection between ego and the mind also reflects the dynamic interplay between conscious and unconscious elements of the psyche. While the ego operates at the level of conscious awareness, it is also influenced by deeper layers of the mind, including subconscious beliefs, fears, and desires that shape behavior and perception. Understanding this interplay is essential for cultivating self-awareness and navigating the complexities of human consciousness.

The connection between ego and the mind highlights the intricate relationship between identity, perception, and self-awareness. By exploring the workings of the mind and unraveling the complexities of ego, individuals can cultivate greater self-awareness, mindfulness, and resilience in navigating the intricacies of human existence. As we delve into the depths of consciousness, may we embrace the transformative power of self-discovery and self-awareness, fostering deeper connections with ourselves and the world around us.

## Using mindfulness to observe and detach from ego-driven thoughts

Using mindfulness to observe and detach from ego-driven thoughts is a transformative practice that allows individuals to cultivate greater self-awareness, emotional resilience, and inner peace. Mindfulness, rooted in present moment awareness and non-judgmental observation, provides a powerful tool for disengaging from the grip of ego-driven narratives and perceptions, fostering a deeper connection with the essence of being.

**Cultivating Present Moment Awareness:**
Mindfulness invites individuals to anchor
their awareness in the present moment,
cultivating a sense of presence and
attentiveness to the unfolding of
experience. By directing attention to the
sensations of the body, the rhythm of the
breath, or the sensory richness of the
present moment, individuals can cultivate
a state of heightened awareness that
transcends the confines of ego-driven
thought patterns.

**Observing Ego-driven Thoughts with
Curiosity and Compassion:** Mindfulness
encourages individuals to observe ego-
driven thoughts with curiosity and
compassion, rather than judgment or

identification. Instead of becoming entangled in the storyline of ego, individuals can step back and observe the transient nature of thoughts and emotions as they arise and pass away. By adopting a stance of compassionate curiosity, individuals can develop a greater understanding of the underlying beliefs and fears that fuel ego-driven patterns of thought.

**Practicing Non-Identification:** Mindfulness teaches individuals to recognize that they are not defined by their thoughts or emotions, including those stemming from the ego. By cultivating a sense of spacious awareness, individuals can observe ego-driven thoughts as passing phenomena without becoming entangled in their narrative or implications. This practice of non-identification allows individuals to create distance from ego-driven patterns of thought, cultivating a sense of inner freedom and detachment.

**Cultivating Acceptance and Non-Resistance:** Mindfulness encourages individuals to cultivate acceptance and non-resistance towards the contents of consciousness, including ego-driven thoughts and emotions. Instead of engaging in a struggle against the ego or attempting to suppress unwanted thoughts, individuals can practice accepting them with open-hearted awareness. This attitude of acceptance creates space for thoughts and emotions to arise and dissolve naturally, without fueling a cycle of reactivity or inner conflict.

**Redirecting Attention to the Present Moment:** Mindfulness empowers individuals to redirect their attention to the present moment whenever they become entangled in ego-driven thought patterns. By shifting focus to the breath, the sensations of the body, or the sights and sounds of the external environment, individuals can disengage from rumination and bring their awareness back to the richness of the present moment. This practice of grounding in the here and now helps individuals break free from the grip of ego-driven narratives and connect with a deeper sense of presence and inner stillness.

Using mindfulness to observe and detach from ego-driven thoughts is a transformative practice that empowers individuals to cultivate greater self-awareness, emotional resilience, and inner peace. By cultivating present moment awareness, observing ego-driven thoughts with curiosity and compassion, practicing non-identification, cultivating acceptance and non-resistance, and redirecting attention to the present moment, individuals can break free from the grip of ego-driven patterns of thought and discover a profound sense of freedom and authenticity in the present moment.

## The benefits of a mindful approach to managing ego

A mindful approach to managing ego offers a myriad of benefits that extend across mental, emotional, and relational dimensions. By cultivating awareness, non-reactivity, and a deeper understanding of the self, individuals can navigate the complexities of ego with greater ease, fostering personal growth and well-being. Here are several key benefits of adopting a mindful approach to managing ego:

**Enhanced Self-Awareness:** Mindfulness shines a light on the intricacies of the mind, unveiling patterns of thought, emotion, and behavior. By observing the ego with non-judgmental awareness, individuals gain insight into the conditioned responses, beliefs, and narratives that shape their self-perception. Enhanced self-awareness becomes a powerful tool for personal growth and transformation, allowing individuals to make conscious choices aligned with their authentic values.

**Reduced Reactivity and Impulsivity:**
Mindfulness teaches individuals to respond to situations with greater awareness and intention, rather than reacting impulsively based on ego-driven patterns. By creating a space between stimulus and response, individuals can break free from habitual reactions rooted in ego and choose more skillful and measured responses. This reduces impulsivity, fosters emotional regulation, and promotes a sense of inner calm and resilience.

**Cultivation of Emotional Resilience:**
Mindfulness enables individuals to navigate challenging emotions with greater resilience and equanimity. Rather than being swept away by the tumult of ego-driven emotions, individuals can observe them with a sense of detachment and acceptance. This capacity to witness

emotions without becoming overwhelmed enhances emotional intelligence, allowing individuals to respond to emotional challenges with greater skill and poise.

**Improved Relationship Dynamics:** A mindful approach to managing ego has positive implications for interpersonal relationships. By cultivating awareness of one's own egoic tendencies, individuals can foster empathy and understanding in their interactions with others. Mindfulness also promotes active listening, non-judgmental communication, and the ability to hold space for diverse perspectives, contributing to healthier and more harmonious relationships.

**Increased Focus and Concentration:** Mindfulness involves training the mind to stay anchored in the present moment, reducing the mental chatter associated with ego-driven thoughts. As a result, individuals experience increased focus and concentration. The ability to direct attention intentionally enhances cognitive functioning, decision-making, and problem-solving skills, leading to improved overall performance in various aspects of life.

**Heightened Creativity and Open-mindedness:** The spacious awareness cultivated through mindfulness creates room for creativity and open-mindedness. By detaching from rigid egoic beliefs and perspectives, individuals become more receptive to new ideas and insights. This openness to possibilities fosters creativity and innovation, allowing individuals to approach challenges with fresh perspectives and adaptive solutions.

**Promotion of Authenticity and Integrity:**
Mindfulness encourages individuals to live
authentically by aligning their actions
with their true values and intentions. By
disentangling from ego-driven desires for
external validation or approval, individuals
can make choices that resonate with
their authentic selves. This authenticity
promotes a sense of integrity and a
deeper connection to one's inner truth.

**Enhanced Stress Management:**
Mindfulness is renowned for its stress-
reducing benefits. By managing ego-driven
thoughts that contribute to stress and
anxiety, individuals can create a more
harmonious relationship with the demands
of life. Mindfulness practices, such as
meditation and deep breathing, activate
the relaxation response, fostering a sense
of calm and balance even in the face of

challenging circumstances.

A mindful approach to managing ego brings a wealth of benefits, ranging from heightened self-awareness and emotional resilience to improved relationships and enhanced cognitive functioning. By incorporating mindfulness into daily life, individuals can foster a sense of inner peace, authenticity, and well-being, navigating the complexities of the ego with wisdom and compassion.

# Chapter 14: Ego and Personal Growth

Ego and Personal Growth embarks on a profound exploration into the intricate dynamics between the ego—a fundamental aspect of human identity—and the journey towards personal evolution and self-discovery. In the realm of psychology and self-awareness, the ego serves as both a guiding force and a potential obstacle to individual growth, shaping perceptions, behaviors, and aspirations along the path of self-realization.

At its core, the ego represents the intricate web of self-perception, identity, and consciousness through which individuals navigate the complexities of human experience. It encompasses the beliefs, values, and narratives that define one's sense of self and shape interactions with the world. The ego plays a pivotal role in the process of personal growth, influencing aspirations, motivations, and the pursuit of fulfillment.

The journey of personal growth unfolds as individuals navigate the terrain of ego, confronting the layers of conditioning, fears, and limitations that inhibit self-realization and authenticity. It involves a process of introspection, self-discovery, and transformation, as individuals strive to transcend the confines of ego-driven patterns and align with their deepest truths and aspirations.

The relationship between ego and personal growth is multifaceted, encompassing both the potential for self-discovery and the challenges of egoic attachments and resistance to change. While the ego often seeks security, validation, and control, personal growth requires a willingness to embrace uncertainty, vulnerability, and the unknown. It entails a journey of exploration and expansion, as individuals confront fears, overcome obstacles, and cultivate resilience in the pursuit of authenticity and fulfillment.

Moreover, personal growth involves a deepening awareness of the interconnectedness of self and others, transcending the boundaries of egoic identity to embrace the shared humanity and collective wisdom of the human experience. It involves cultivating empathy, compassion, and authenticity in relationships, fostering a sense of belonging and interconnectedness that transcends the limitations of ego-driven separation and division.

Ego and Personal Growth invites individuals to embark on a transformative journey of self-discovery, empowerment, and authenticity. It explores the complexities of ego and its impact on the process of personal evolution, while illuminating the pathways to self-realization, fulfillment, and connection with oneself and the world. As individuals navigate the intricate interplay between ego and personal growth, may they embrace the transformative power of self-awareness, resilience, and authenticity, forging deeper connections with themselves and the world around them.



Ego, while an integral aspect of human consciousness, can also serve as a significant barrier to personal growth and development. Rooted in the need for self-preservation, validation, and control, the ego often manifests in patterns of thought and behavior that inhibit self-awareness, resilience, and authentic self-expression. Here's how ego can hinder personal growth and development:

**Resistance to Change:** The ego is inherently resistant to change, seeking comfort, security, and familiarity in the status quo. It clings to familiar beliefs, identities, and behaviors, even if they no longer serve the individual's growth and well-being. This resistance to change can prevent individuals from stepping outside their comfort zones, taking risks, and embracing new opportunities for growth and self-discovery.

**Attachment to Identity and Labels:** Ego is deeply intertwined with identity, attaching significance to labels, roles, and external markers of success and validation. Individuals may become overly attached to identities based on societal expectations, achievements, or social status, defining themselves solely by external factors rather than their intrinsic worth and potential. This attachment to identity can limit self-exploration and experimentation, constraining individuals within rigid roles and expectations that stifle personal growth and authenticity.

**Fear of Failure and Rejection:** Ego is often driven by a fear of failure, rejection, or inadequacy, leading individuals to avoid taking risks or pursuing their aspirations. The ego perceives failure as a threat to its sense of identity and self-worth, triggering feelings of shame, insecurity, and self-doubt. As a result, individuals may resist challenges, play it safe, and remain within their comfort zones, missing out on opportunities for growth, resilience, and self-empowerment.

**Comparisons and Competition:** Ego thrives on comparisons and competition, fueling a perpetual cycle of comparison with others and striving for superiority or validation. Individuals may measure their worth and success based on external benchmarks, constantly seeking validation and recognition from others. This constant comparison breeds insecurity, envy, and resentment, detracting from genuine self-awareness, fulfillment, and connection with oneself and others.

**Defensive Patterns and Resistance to Feedback:** Ego often manifests in defensive patterns of thought and behavior, resisting feedback, criticism, or challenges to its sense of self. Individuals may become defensive or reactive when confronted with differing perspectives or constructive criticism, perceiving it as a threat to their egoic identity. This defensiveness hinders self-reflection, learning, and growth, preventing individuals from embracing opportunities for self-improvement and personal development.

**Limited Perspective and Closed-mindedness:** Ego tends to operate within a limited perspective, filtering perceptions and experiences through the lens of self-interest and self-preservation. Individuals may become closed-minded or rigid in their beliefs, dismissing alternative viewpoints or new ideas that challenge their existing worldview. This closed-mindedness inhibits curiosity, exploration, and intellectual growth, preventing individuals from expanding their horizons and embracing the diversity of human experience.

Ego can hinder personal growth and development by fostering resistance to change, attachment to identity, fear of failure, comparisons, defensive patterns, and closed-mindedness. By cultivating self-awareness, humility, and openness to growth, individuals can transcend the limitations of ego and embrace a journey of self-discovery, resilience, and authentic self-expression. As individuals confront the barriers imposed by ego, may they cultivate the courage and resilience to embark on a transformative journey of personal growth, empowerment, and fulfillment.

## Overcoming ego to embrace change and new experiences

Overcoming ego to embrace change and new experiences is a transformative journey of self-awareness, resilience, and personal growth. It involves cultivating the courage to transcend ego-driven patterns of thought and behavior, and to embrace uncertainty, vulnerability, and the unknown. Here are some strategies for overcoming ego and embracing change:

**Cultivate Self-Awareness:** The first step in overcoming ego is to cultivate self-awareness. This involves observing the thoughts, emotions, and beliefs that arise within the mind without judgment or attachment. By developing a deeper understanding of the ego's patterns and tendencies, individuals can begin to recognize when ego-driven resistance arises in the face of change.

**Practice Mindfulness:** Mindfulness is a

powerful tool for overcoming ego and embracing change. By cultivating present-moment awareness and non-judgmental observation, individuals can create space between themselves and their ego-driven thoughts and emotions. Mindfulness practices such as meditation, breathwork, and body scans can help individuals develop greater clarity, resilience, and acceptance in the face of change.

**Challenge Limiting Beliefs:** Ego often thrives on limiting beliefs and self-imposed limitations that prevent individuals from embracing new experiences and opportunities. By challenging these beliefs and questioning the validity of ego-driven narratives, individuals can expand their sense of possibility and potential. This involves reframing negative self-talk, embracing a growth mindset, and cultivating a sense of curiosity and openness to new possibilities.

**Embrace Vulnerability:** Embracing change requires a willingness to embrace vulnerability and step outside of one's comfort zone. Vulnerability involves acknowledging and accepting the inherent uncertainty and impermanence of life, and being willing to take risks and face challenges with courage and resilience. By embracing vulnerability, individuals can cultivate a sense of authenticity, connection, and growth in the face of change.

**Cultivate Flexibility and Adaptability:** Overcoming ego involves cultivating flexibility and adaptability in response to changing circumstances and experiences.

Instead of clinging to rigid expectations or attachments to outcomes, individuals can practice surrendering to the flow of life and adapting to new situations with grace and resilience. This requires letting go of the need for control and embracing the inherent fluidity and unpredictability of life's journey.

**Seek Growth Opportunities:** Embracing change requires actively seeking out growth opportunities and new experiences that challenge and stretch one's comfort zone. This may involve trying new activities, learning new skills, or exploring unfamiliar perspectives and cultures. By embracing a spirit of curiosity and adventure, individuals can expand their horizons, cultivate resilience, and discover new aspects of themselves in the process.

**Practice Self-Compassion:** Finally, overcoming ego and embracing change requires practicing self-compassion and kindness towards oneself. Change can be challenging and uncomfortable, and it's important to treat oneself with gentleness and understanding during times of transition. By offering oneself the same compassion and support that one would offer to a friend, individuals can navigate the ups and downs of change with greater resilience and self-acceptance.

Overcoming ego to embrace change and new experiences is a transformative journey of self-discovery, resilience, and personal growth. By cultivating self-awareness, mindfulness, vulnerability, flexibility, and self-compassion, individuals can transcend ego-driven resistance and open themselves to the richness and possibility of life's unfolding journey. As individuals embrace the transformative power of change, may they discover new depths of resilience, authenticity, and fulfillment in the process.

## The role of vulnerability and humility in personal growth

The role of vulnerability and humility in personal growth is profound and transformative, shaping individuals' journeys towards self-discovery, resilience, and authenticity. Vulnerability and humility serve as catalysts for growth by fostering openness, connection, and a willingness to embrace the full spectrum of human experience. Here's how vulnerability and humility contribute to personal growth:

**Opening the Heart:** Vulnerability involves the willingness to open one's heart and expose oneself to the full range of emotions, including fear, uncertainty, and discomfort. By allowing oneself to be vulnerable, individuals create space for genuine connection and intimacy with themselves and others. This openness fosters deeper relationships, empathy, and understanding, creating a foundation for personal growth and transformation.

**Cultivating Authenticity:** Vulnerability and humility encourage individuals to embrace their authentic selves, flaws and all. Rather than hiding behind masks of perfection or self-protection, individuals who embrace vulnerability are willing to show up as they are, with courage and authenticity. This authenticity cultivates a sense of integrity, self-acceptance, and inner peace, allowing individuals to live in alignment with their deepest values and aspirations.

**Fostering Resilience:** Vulnerability and humility are essential ingredients in building resilience and inner strength. By facing fears and embracing vulnerability, individuals develop the resilience to navigate life's challenges and setbacks with courage and grace. Rather than seeing vulnerability as a sign of weakness, they recognize it as a source of strength and empowerment, allowing them to bounce back from adversity with greater wisdom and resilience.

**Facilitating Learning and Growth:** Humility involves an openness to learning and growth, recognizing that true wisdom lies in acknowledging one's limitations and embracing the insights and perspectives of others. By approaching life with humility, individuals cultivate a growth mindset that embraces challenges, setbacks, and failures as opportunities for learning and self-improvement. This openness to growth fosters a spirit of curiosity, creativity, and innovation, allowing individuals to expand their horizons and reach their full potential.

**Cultivating Empathy and Compassion:** Vulnerability and humility deepen individuals' capacity for empathy and compassion towards themselves and others. By acknowledging their own vulnerabilities and imperfections, individuals develop greater empathy and understanding towards the struggles and challenges faced by others. This empathy fosters deeper connections and a sense of shared humanity, creating a ripple effect of kindness, compassion, and healing in the world.

**Promoting Authentic Connection:** Vulnerability and humility create the conditions for authentic connection and belonging in relationships. When individuals are willing to show up authentically and vulnerably, they invite others to do the same. This fosters genuine connections built on trust, mutual respect, and emotional intimacy, enriching individuals' lives with meaningful relationships and a sense of belonging.

The role of vulnerability and humility in personal growth is multifaceted and profound. By embracing vulnerability, cultivating humility, and embracing the full spectrum of human experience, individuals can embark on a transformative journey of self-discovery, resilience, and authenticity. As they open their hearts, minds, and spirits to the richness of vulnerability and humility, may they discover new depths of connection, resilience, and fulfillment in their lives.

# Chapter 15: Letting Go of Ego

In the pursuit of personal and spiritual growth, the concept of "Letting Go of Ego" emerges as a fundamental principle, inviting individuals on a transformative journey of self-discovery, liberation, and authenticity. Ego, often characterized as the construct of self-perception and identity, plays a central role in shaping individuals' thoughts, behaviors, and relationships with themselves and others. However, the very nature of ego, with its attachments, fears, and illusions, can serve as a barrier to inner peace, fulfillment, and genuine connection.

"Letting Go of Ego" is not a mere act of

renunciation or denial, but rather a profound process of liberation and awakening to the essence of being. It involves releasing attachments to external identities, narratives, and desires that obscure the deeper truth of one's existence. By relinquishing the grip of ego-driven patterns of thought and behavior, individuals open themselves to the boundless possibilities of self-discovery, connection, and spiritual awakening.

The journey of letting go of ego begins with a willingness to explore the depths of one's consciousness and confront the illusions and limitations of egoic perception. It requires cultivating a spirit of humility, openness, and curiosity towards the inner landscape of the mind and heart. Through practices such as mindfulness, self-inquiry, and introspection, individuals embark on a journey of self-discovery, unraveling the layers of conditioning, fears, and attachments that bind them to the confines of ego.

As individuals traverse the path of letting go of ego, they encounter moments of discomfort, uncertainty, and vulnerability. Yet, it is within these moments of surrender and release that the seeds of transformation and awakening are sown. By embracing the present moment with openness and acceptance, individuals cultivate a deeper sense of presence, authenticity, and connection with themselves and the world around them.

The process of letting go of ego is not without its challenges and obstacles. It requires courage, patience, and a willingness to confront the shadows and uncertainties that lie within. Yet, it is through the act of letting go that individuals discover the profound freedom and liberation that arises from embracing the fullness of their being.

It is a transformative journey of self-discovery, liberation, and awakening to the essence of who we truly are. It is a journey of releasing attachments, fears, and illusions that obscure the radiant truth of our existence. As individuals surrender to the flow of life and embrace the boundless possibilities of self-discovery and spiritual awakening, may they find the profound peace, joy, and fulfillment that arises from letting go of ego and embracing the infinite expanse of their true selves.

The process of releasing ego and its hold on us is a profound and transformative journey of self-discovery, liberation, and spiritual awakening. It involves unraveling the layers of conditioning, fears, and attachments that bind us to the confines of egoic perception and identity, and embracing the deeper truth of our existence. Here's a closer look at the process of releasing ego and its hold on us:

**Cultivating Self-Awareness:** The first step in releasing ego is cultivating self-awareness. This involves observing the thoughts, emotions, and beliefs that arise within us without judgment or attachment. By developing a deeper understanding of the patterns and tendencies of the ego, we begin to recognize its influence on our thoughts, behaviors, and relationships.

**Practicing Mindfulness:** Mindfulness is a powerful practice for releasing ego and cultivating presence and awareness in the present moment. Through mindfulness meditation, breathwork, and body awareness practices, we learn to observe the fluctuations of the mind and detach from ego-driven thoughts and emotions. By anchoring ourselves in the present moment, we create space for clarity, insight, and inner peace to emerge.

**Letting Go of Attachments:** Ego thrives on attachments—to identities, roles, possessions, and outcomes—that reinforce its sense of self-importance and control. The process of releasing ego involves letting go of these attachments and surrendering to the flow of life. By relinquishing our attachment to external forms of validation and security, we open ourselves to a deeper sense of inner freedom and fulfillment.

**Embracing Vulnerability:** Releasing ego requires a willingness to embrace vulnerability and authenticity in our interactions with ourselves and others. Vulnerability involves acknowledging our imperfections, fears, and insecurities without shame or judgment. By embracing vulnerability, we create space for genuine connection, empathy, and compassion to flourish.

**Cultivating Humility:** Humility is a cornerstone of releasing ego and embracing the interconnectedness of all beings. Humility involves recognizing our interconnectedness with the web of life and acknowledging the contributions of others to our growth and well-being. By cultivating humility, we transcend the limitations of egoic separation and open ourselves to the wisdom and beauty of the world around us.

**Practicing Surrender and Acceptance:** Releasing ego requires a willingness to surrender to the flow of life and accept things as they are. This involves letting go of the need for control, certainty, and perfection, and embracing the inherent uncertainty and impermanence of existence. By practicing surrender and acceptance, we find peace and contentment in the present moment, regardless of external circumstances.

**Cultivating Compassion and Love:**
Releasing ego involves cultivating compassion and love towards ourselves and others. Compassion involves extending kindness, understanding, and forgiveness to ourselves and others, recognizing the shared humanity and inherent worthiness of all beings. By cultivating compassion and love, we dissolve the barriers of egoic separation and connect with the deeper essence of our shared humanity.

The process of releasing ego and its hold on us is a journey of self-discovery, liberation, and spiritual awakening. It involves cultivating self-awareness, practicing mindfulness, letting go of attachments, embracing vulnerability, cultivating humility, practicing surrender and acceptance, and cultivating compassion and love. As we embark on this transformative journey, may we find freedom, peace, and fulfillment in releasing ego and embracing the boundless expanse of our true selves.



Cultivating humility and self-awareness is a transformative journey that requires dedication, practice, and a willingness to explore the depths of one's inner landscape. These practices invite individuals to embrace vulnerability, authenticity, and openness as they deepen their connection with themselves and the world around them. Here are some effective practices for cultivating humility and self-awareness:

**Mindfulness Meditation:** Mindfulness meditation is a powerful practice for cultivating self-awareness and humility. By bringing attention to the present moment with openness and curiosity, individuals learn to observe their thoughts, emotions, and sensations without judgment or attachment. Regular meditation practice helps individuals develop a deeper understanding of the patterns of the mind and cultivate a sense of inner calm and clarity.

**Journaling and Reflection:** Journaling and reflection are valuable tools for exploring one's thoughts, emotions, and experiences. By writing down thoughts and feelings in a journal, individuals gain insight into their inner landscape and patterns of behavior. Reflection prompts such as "what am I grateful for?" or "what challenges have I faced today?" can deepen self-awareness and foster a sense of humility and gratitude.

**Seeking Feedback and Input:** Seeking feedback and input from others is an important practice for cultivating humility and self-awareness. By actively listening to the perspectives and insights of others, individuals gain valuable insights into their blind spots, strengths, and areas for growth. Constructive feedback serves as a mirror that reflects back our strengths and weaknesses, helping us cultivate humility and self-awareness.

**Practicing Gratitude:** Cultivating gratitude is a powerful practice for fostering humility and self-awareness. By acknowledging the blessings and abundance in our lives, individuals cultivate a sense of humility and appreciation for the interconnectedness of all beings. Gratitude practices such as keeping a gratitude journal, expressing thanks to others, or reflecting on moments of joy and beauty help individuals cultivate a sense of humility and contentment.

**Embracing Vulnerability:** Embracing vulnerability is an essential practice for cultivating humility and self-awareness. By acknowledging our imperfections, fears, and insecurities, individuals create space for genuine connection and authenticity. Practices such as sharing vulnerably with trusted friends or loved ones, expressing emotions authentically, and acknowledging mistakes and failures help individuals cultivate humility and resilience.

**Cultivating Compassion and Empathy:** Cultivating compassion and empathy towards ourselves and others is a foundational practice for fostering humility and self-awareness. By recognizing the shared humanity and inherent worthiness of all beings, individuals cultivate a sense of humility and interconnectedness. Practices such as loving-kindness meditation, acts of kindness and service, and empathetic listening help individuals cultivate compassion and empathy in their daily lives.

**Engaging in Self-Reflection and Inquiry:**
Engaging in self-reflection and inquiry is a transformative practice for deepening self-awareness and cultivating humility. By asking reflective questions such as "who am I?" or "what do I value most?" individuals gain insight into their core beliefs, values, and aspirations. Self-inquiry practices such as contemplative walks in nature, silent retreats, or guided introspection exercises help individuals cultivate a sense of humility and inner wisdom.

Cultivating humility and self-awareness is a lifelong journey of exploration and discovery. By embracing practices such as mindfulness meditation, journaling and reflection, seeking feedback and input, practicing gratitude, embracing vulnerability, cultivating compassion and empathy, and engaging in self-reflection and inquiry, individuals deepen their connection with themselves and the world around them. As they cultivate humility and self-awareness, may they discover greater clarity, authenticity, and fulfillment in their lives.

## The freedom and peace that comes with letting go of ego

The freedom and peace that come with letting go of ego are profound and transformative, offering individuals a pathway to liberation, authenticity, and inner harmony. As individuals release the grip of ego-driven patterns and attachments, they discover a sense of spaciousness, ease, and contentment that transcends the limitations of the self. Here's a closer look at the freedom and peace that accompany letting go of ego:

**Release from Mental Prison:** Letting go of ego liberates individuals from the confines of the mental prison created by self-limiting beliefs, fears, and attachments. Rather than being bound by the dictates of egoic conditioning, individuals experience a sense of expansiveness and freedom that allows them to explore the boundless possibilities of existence.

**Embrace of Inner Peace:** The release of ego brings about a profound sense of inner peace and tranquility. As individuals relinquish the need for control, validation, and external approval, they discover a deep wellspring of peace that arises from within. This inner peace serves as a sanctuary amidst the turbulence of life's challenges and uncertainties, providing a stable anchor amidst the ebb and flow of existence.

**Alignment with Authenticity:** Letting go of ego aligns individuals with their authentic selves—the essence of who they truly are beyond the trappings of egoic identity and perception. By embracing authenticity, individuals cultivate a sense of integrity, wholeness, and alignment with their deepest values and aspirations. This alignment brings a profound sense of fulfillment and purpose, as individuals live in alignment with their truest selves.

**Connection with Others:** The release of ego fosters deeper connections and relationships with others based on authenticity, empathy, and genuine connection. As individuals let go of the need for superiority, validation, and competition, they create space for authentic connections grounded in mutual respect, understanding, and compassion. This deepening of relationships brings a sense of belonging and interconnectedness that enriches individuals' lives with meaning and significance.

**Embrace of Impermanence:** Letting go of ego allows individuals to embrace the impermanence and transience of life with grace and acceptance. Rather than clinging to attachments and resisting change, individuals cultivate a sense of equanimity and surrender that allows them to flow with the ever-changing currents of existence. This embrace of impermanence brings a profound sense of liberation and freedom from the suffering caused by attachment and resistance.

**Experience of Joy and Gratitude:** The release of ego opens individuals to the experience of joy, gratitude, and appreciation for the richness and beauty of life. By cultivating a mindset of gratitude and presence, individuals discover moments of awe, wonder, and beauty in the ordinary moments of everyday life. This cultivation of joy and gratitude brings a deep sense of fulfillment and contentment that transcends external circumstances and conditions.

The freedom and peace that come with letting go of ego are transformative and liberating. As individuals release the grip of ego-driven patterns and attachments, they discover a profound sense of inner peace, authenticity, and connection with themselves and the world around them.

In the embrace of authenticity, joy, and gratitude, individuals discover a pathway to liberation, fulfillment, and wholeness that enriches every aspect of their lives.

# Reflections: Living with a Healthy Ego

Here we delves into the intricate balance between self-confidence, self-awareness, and humility, fostering a harmonious relationship with one's sense of self. In a world where ego is often portrayed negatively, the concept of a healthy ego emerges as a vital component of personal growth, resilience, and well-being. It embodies a state of equilibrium where individuals navigate the complexities of life with confidence, authenticity, and grace.

At its core, a healthy ego represents a balanced sense of self-esteem and self-worth that is rooted in self-awareness and genuine acceptance of one's strengths and limitations. It involves embracing a realistic and compassionate view of oneself while maintaining a growth-oriented mindset that welcomes opportunities for learning and self-improvement.

Living with a healthy ego involves cultivating a deep understanding of oneself, recognizing individual talents, passions, and values, and leveraging them to pursue meaningful goals and aspirations. It entails celebrating achievements and successes while also acknowledging setbacks and challenges as opportunities for growth and resilience.

A healthy ego fosters authentic connections and relationships with others, grounded in mutual respect, empathy, and understanding. It involves honoring the unique perspectives and experiences of others while maintaining healthy boundaries and assertiveness in communication and interactions.

Living with a healthy ego is about embracing the fullness of one's humanity—the strengths, vulnerabilities, joys, and struggles—while navigating life with integrity, authenticity, and compassion. It is a journey of self-discovery, growth, and empowerment that allows individuals to thrive in a world that celebrates diversity, resilience, and the richness of the human experience. Through the exploration of living with a healthy ego, individuals uncover a pathway to fulfillment, connection, and well-being that resonates deeply with their truest selves.



In reflecting on the journey explored throughout this book, several key points and takeaways emerge, offering profound insights into the nature of ego, personal growth, and the pursuit of authenticity. Here's a recap of the key points and takeaways:

**Understanding the Nature of Ego:** Ego is a multifaceted construct that influences our thoughts, behaviors, and relationships. It can manifest in various forms, including inflated, fragile, or healthy, each shaping our perceptions of self and the world.

**The Impact of Ego on Relationships:** Ego

plays a pivotal role in shaping our interactions with others. From romantic relationships to friendships and family dynamics, ego-driven patterns can either foster connection and understanding or breed conflict and disconnection.

**Navigating Success and Failure:** Ego influences our attitudes toward success and failure. While an inflated ego may lead to arrogance and entitlement in success, a fragile ego may crumble in the face of failure. Cultivating humility and resilience can help navigate the highs and lows of life with grace and integrity.

**Cultivating Self-Awareness and Authenticity:** Self-awareness is key to transcending ego-driven patterns and embracing authenticity. Through mindfulness, reflection, and introspection, individuals can uncover their true selves and live in alignment with their values and aspirations.

**Embracing Vulnerability and Humility:** Vulnerability and humility are essential components of personal growth and connection. By embracing vulnerability, individuals cultivate empathy, resilience, and genuine relationships grounded in authenticity and compassion.

**Finding Peace in Letting Go:** Letting go of ego is a transformative journey toward inner peace and liberation. By releasing attachments, embracing impermanence, and practicing acceptance, individuals discover a profound sense of freedom and contentment in the present moment.

**Living with a Healthy Ego:** Cultivating a healthy ego involves finding balance between self-assuredness and humility, confidence and compassion. It entails acknowledging one's worth and strengths while remaining open to growth, learning, and connection with others.

The journey of exploring ego and personal growth is a profound and transformative one. It invites individuals to delve into the depths of their being, confront the illusions of ego, and embrace the richness of authentic living. Through self-awareness, vulnerability, and humility, individuals can transcend ego-driven patterns and cultivate a sense of peace, purpose, and connection that enriches every aspect of their lives. As we continue on our journeys, may we embody the wisdom and insights gleaned from exploring the complexities of ego and embrace the path of authenticity, resilience, and inner harmony.

## The importance of maintaining a healthy balance of ego in our lives

Maintaining a healthy balance of ego in our lives is crucial for fostering well-being, positive relationships, and personal growth. Ego, often viewed as the sense of self and identity, influences how we perceive ourselves and interact with the world. While ego can empower us with confidence and self-assurance, an imbalance can lead to arrogance, insecurity, and disconnection from others. Here's why maintaining a healthy balance of ego is essential:

**Self-Confidence and Self-Worth:** A healthy ego cultivates a sense of self-confidence and self-worth. It allows us to acknowledge our strengths, talents, and accomplishments without veering into arrogance or narcissism. With a healthy sense of self-esteem, we can navigate life's challenges with resilience and optimism.

**Respect for Others:** Maintaining a healthy balance of ego involves recognizing the value and worth of others. It entails humility and empathy, acknowledging that everyone's experiences, perspectives, and contributions are valid and deserving of respect. By cultivating humility, we foster harmonious relationships built on mutual understanding and appreciation.

**Openness to Growth and Learning:** A healthy ego is characterized by openness to growth and learning. It involves acknowledging our limitations, embracing feedback and constructive criticism, and being receptive to new ideas and perspectives. By remaining humble and curious, we create opportunities for personal and professional development.

**Emotional Regulation and Resilience:** Maintaining a healthy balance of ego contributes to emotional regulation and resilience. It allows us to navigate setbacks, failures, and disappointments with grace and equanimity. Rather than being consumed by ego-driven emotions such as pride or shame, we can approach challenges with humility and resilience, finding strength in adversity.

**Authenticity and Integrity:** A healthy ego aligns with authenticity and integrity. It involves living in alignment with our values, beliefs, and aspirations, rather than seeking validation or approval from external sources. By embracing authenticity, we cultivate a deep sense of inner harmony and fulfillment, free from the pressures of ego-driven expectations.

**Positive Impact on Relationships:** Maintaining a healthy balance of ego enhances the quality of our relationships. It fosters empathy, compassion, and genuine connection with others, leading to deeper intimacy and trust. By prioritizing humility and understanding in our interactions, we create a supportive and nurturing environment where everyone feels valued and respected.

**Contributing to Collective Well-Being:** A healthy balance of ego contributes to collective well-being and social harmony. It promotes cooperation, collaboration, and empathy, fostering a sense of community and belonging. By transcending ego-driven divisions and conflicts, we can work together to create a more inclusive, compassionate, and equitable society.

Maintaining a healthy balance of ego is essential for fostering personal fulfillment, positive relationships, and collective well-being. It involves cultivating self-confidence while remaining humble, respecting the perspectives of others, and embracing opportunities for growth and learning. By prioritizing authenticity, empathy, and integrity in our lives, we can cultivate a healthy ego that enriches our experiences and contributes to a more harmonious and compassionate world.



In the pursuit of living a fulfilling and authentic life with a healthy ego, it's essential to recognize that the journey is as significant as the destination. It's a continuous process of self-discovery, growth, and refinement—a journey that unfolds with each moment, experience, and interaction. Here are some final thoughts on embracing this journey:

**Embrace Self-Compassion:** As we navigate the complexities of ego and authenticity, it's crucial to extend self-compassion and kindness to ourselves. Acknowledge that perfection is not the goal, and that setbacks and challenges are natural parts of the journey. Treat yourself with the same understanding and empathy that you would offer to a friend.

**Cultivate Mindfulness and Presence:** Living with a healthy ego requires cultivating mindfulness and presence in our daily lives. By being fully present in each moment, we can observe the fluctuations of the ego without becoming entangled in them. Mindfulness practices such as meditation, deep breathing, and conscious awareness help us stay grounded and centered amidst the ups and downs of life.

**Nurture Authentic Connections:** Authenticity thrives in the soil of genuine connections and relationships. Nurture connections with those who uplift and support you on your journey, and be willing to offer the same support and encouragement in return. Authentic connections remind us of our shared humanity and inspire us to live with integrity and purpose.

**Practice Gratitude and Appreciation:** Cultivating gratitude and appreciation enriches our experience of life and deepens our sense of fulfillment. Take time each day to reflect on the blessings and gifts in your life, no matter how small. By practicing gratitude, we shift our focus from scarcity to abundance, fostering a sense of contentment and joy.

**Embrace Vulnerability and Courage:** Authentic living requires vulnerability and courage—the willingness to show up, be seen, and embrace the fullness of our humanity. Embrace vulnerability as a gateway to deeper connections, creativity, and growth. Know that it takes courage to live authentically, but the rewards are profound and transformative.

**Celebrate Your Journey:** Celebrate the milestones, breakthroughs, and moments of growth along your journey. Each step forward, no matter how small, is a testament to your courage, resilience, and commitment to living authentically. Celebrate your progress and honor the lessons learned along the way.

**Stay Open to Possibility:** Finally, stay open to the endless possibilities that life has to offer. The journey of living authentically with a healthy ego is dynamic and ever-evolving. Stay curious, embrace change, and trust in the wisdom of your own inner guidance. Remember that the path to fulfillment is uniquely yours, and it unfolds with each choice you make and each moment you embrace.

In closing, living a fulfilling and authentic life with a healthy ego is a journey of self-discovery, growth, and empowerment. It's about embracing the fullness of who you are, honoring your truth, and living in alignment with your deepest values and aspirations. As you continue on your journey, may you cultivate compassion, courage, and gratitude, and may you find fulfillment and joy in every step along the way.